979.4

Women of the
GOLD RUSH

Women of the
GOLD RUSH

Elisabeth Margo

Indian Head Books
New York

To Dorothy and Albert Margo

I wish to thank Professor Edward Eugene Robinson of Stanford University for his generous and scholarly advice; Ned Bradford for technical assistance; Professor William B. Hesseltine of the University of Wisconsin for provocative suggestions; and Professor Frank Freidel of Harvard University for his unstinting help and encouragement. I also owe a debt of gratitude to the staffs of the Huntington Library, Bancroft Library, University of Southern California Library, and the Stanford University Library for their kindness in making this material available to me.

Originally published as *Taming the Forty-Niner*

Copyright © 1955 by Elisabeth Margo Freidel
All rights reserved.

This edition published by Indian Head Books,
a division of Barnes & Noble, Inc.,
by arrangement with Henry Holt & Company.

1992 Indian Head Books

ISBN 1-56619-064-9

Printed and bound in the United States of America

M 9 8 7 6 5 4 3 2 1

CONTENTS

PART ONE

The Big Stag Party

CHAPTER *1*

Seeing the Elephant

Just over a hundred years ago there was a story going the rounds about a farmer who set his heart on seeing the elephant. Like most nineteenth century humor, it doesn't seem funny now, but it was both funny and important—and even a little gruesome—in 1849.

This farmer heard one day that the circus would be coming to a neighboring city, and with the circus would be a real elephant. All his life he had heard of this fabulous beast, and the desire to see one grew in him and troubled him mightily. He set out for town with his wagon loaded with goods for the market. As he neared the town, he came upon the circus menagerie traveling towards him.

His horses reared in fright, his wagon turned over in the ditch, his eggs were smashed and he himself was battered and bruised. But he rose from the ruins triumphant.

"A fig for the damage," he cried, "for I have seen the elephant!"

Both the forty-niners and the men who stayed home saw in this story a symbol of the gold rush; "seeing the elephant" became contemporary slang for going to California. But the difference between the two kinds of men—the seekers and the stayers—was that the stayers saw principally the shattered wagon and the broken eggs, while the seekers saw above all the glory of beholding the elephant.

This difference in point of view is crucial. It was one of the conditions of that vast natural experiment in social psychology which historians call the gold rush.

When a scientist experiments, he sets certain conditions for his experiment, adds other known factors and observes the result of the combination. Out of known plus known comes the unknown, a new entity. The conditions out of which gold rush society arose, though set by historical accident and not by the scientist, were as specific and definite as the conditions of any laboratory experiment.

The conditions were these: time, place, people, and the great catalytic event that started the interaction of time, place and people.

The time was the later forties, a period full of wars and echoes of wars, stories of filibustering expeditions, tales of adventure in far places. Europe seethed with the great wars of 1848, and, erupting, threw refugees to American shores like pumice flying from a volcano. Eastern Americans sat at home and read of the adventures of other Americans in the Mexican War. The coming North-South hostility simmered. Manifest Destiny was like an odor in the air people breathed. And over all and through all was restlessness and a vague unquiet craving for adventure.

The place was California—northern California, that started at San Francisco, led up the rivers to Sacramento and Stockton, and forked out and up into a widespread net of camps along the ravines of the many-branched Sierra Nevada creeks.

The country was sometimes beautiful in a way new to Eastern eyes, and sometimes harsh and forbidding: higher in its mountains, wetter in its rains and floods, dryer in its parching valley summers, emptier and broader and taller, nakeder in its bare hills and more imposing in its huge redwood forests, wilder in its wilderness and teeming with strange crowds in its cities: altogether more of everything than Easterners were used to. Before the gold hunters in-

4

vaded like a swarm of locusts, the state was relatively uninhabited, possessed only by the fringe of Spanish Californians and Indians and American soldiers along the coast of the Pacific. A war had been fought to win it for the United States, and a few pioneers had filtered in, but until 1848 California meant nothing to most Americans but a faraway scrap of Manifest Destiny. Abruptly in the fall of 1848, California became a great golden magnet pulling at the minds of men.

It was in June of that year that John Marshall found gold in Captain Sutter's millrace. Before the year was out, the word had gone around the world and the Argonauts were on their way.

The discovery of gold was the critical event that brought these particular people to this place at this time, determined what manner of people came and what kind of place they found when they got there.

There was gold—gold lying loose in the mountain ravines, gold for the taking, free and for nothing—nothing but heartache and backbreaking work. It belonged to no one, and it might as well belong to you. It lay there, up in the canyons, far back in the mountains, waiting for you like buried treasure in a pirate story, but not just a little box of it somewhere twenty paces south of a twisted oak —on the contrary, miles and miles of it. It needed only to be sought, dug, panned out, and it was yours.

If you sat in an office in an Eastern city, if you followed the plow on a stony New England farm, if you were a young lawyer just starting practice or a clerk in a shipping house, and if all at once all your sane and solid properties—job, house, wife, family— looked pale and dull to you in the glare of the golden light from the West, you could do as gamblers have always done. You could take wife, family, job and home, security and comfort, and stake them all on a single card, double or nothing. You sold what you could to pay for your passage, and you headed West. There the smiling and implacable dealer slowly laid his cards on the table. If his card came up first, it was all gone for nothing. You had seen the elephant and you were thoroughly broken, you had—as they said—"nary a red." But if your card turned up on the green baize table, you struck it rich in El Dorado and came home a hero, to reclaim all that was yours before you left and add to it your golden pile.

The odds were with the dealer. They always are. The kind of man who went to California knew this and went anyway.

Here then is another condition of the great experiment: the man who joined the gold rush was a gambling man. Perhaps he had never played so much as a game of seven-up, but he was a gambling man in his heart, or he would have stayed home. The Argonaut was an entirely different character from the normal pioneer. There were pioneers in '49 too—westering men, the kind that had always headed for the frontier and always would, and certainly they came into California in larger numbers during those years, as the trail became a well-beaten path. They too had their fling at gold hunting, but in the end they continued to pioneer as they always had with farms and gardens and homes. The Argonaut was something else again. The pioneer brought his family; the Argonaut did not. Many of the gold hunters had good reasons for wanting to get away from it all— unhappy marriages, failures at home, conflicts with society. The Argonaut was strictly off on a big treasure hunt and not at all interested in settling the state. Often he stayed to do so, but it was not his original intent. He intended to strike it rich and go home in a year or two, where everyone would be appropriately dazzled.

It was the Argonaut, not the pioneer, who set the tone and tempo of gold rush society. Within each one of these men, the little boy who played at treasure hunting in his back yard still lived, and now circumstances had given him the chance to live his dream out with the man's strong frame at his disposal and real treasure as the prize. This was the great leveler among the forty-niners. They were by definition —the conditions of the game defined them—that particular combination: the dreamer who is also a man of action, the gambler, adventurer, eternal plunger.

Within this uniformity was tremendous diversity in all other respects. The gold fever plucked men from all walks of life: professional men, farmers, ruffians, ministers, Yankee traders. It drew men from many regions—France, Germany, Australia, China, Latin America—many cultures, many highly various backgrounds. A boy in his twenties who had grown up on a Connecticut farm and had never seen anything but Yankees now walked the muddy alleys of San Francisco jostled by Mexicans, Chinese and river-boat gamblers, seeing hardly one face in twenty that looked like the faces he had seen all his life before. Most Americans of that time led a highly provincial existence. Now they were plunged into a society as diverse and cosmopolitan as any time or place could provide. In the process many of them discovered that social rules which they had taken for granted as God-given were ignored or unknown by many other men, and for the first time came a glimmering of the relativity of morals and conventions.

The whole upheaval had many of the social effects of a troop movement, a war on foreign soil without the fighting.

These were the people: the one essential unity of them, the spirit of treasure hunting, and the inexhaustible variety of race, education, background and culture.

If you had asked these men what they wanted above all else, they would have told you: gold. This was not, however, what they wanted most of all. Men whose driving force is the desire to amass a great

7

fortune go about it otherwise. The Argonaut was as different from the robber baron as he was from the pioneer. He thought he wanted treasure more than anything, but what he really wanted was the excitement, the thrill of seeking.

If you ask a man who fishes all day along an icy creek in the Sierra Nevada what he is after, he will tell you: fish. But if he truly wanted fish, he would buy them. He wants the fun of fishing, and the Argonaut wanted the glory and the adventure of seeking. If he had wanted wealth primarily, he would not have thrown his gold away at the monte table and in the faro rooms of San Francisco. He would not have used his dust—as he characteristically did—for a glorious week end on the town. To him it seemed the supply was inexhaustible and there would always be time—another month, another year—to make that pile for keeps, and hang on to it, but what he wanted right now was to invest it all in one tremendous skyrocket of a Saturday night.

His notion of the proper way to do this differed not at all from what man's notion has always been and still is: liquor, roistering, partying and—given the special circumstances of the times—gambling.

And women?

One primary condition of the great experiment was the woman problem. The first fact about this—first in point of time—was: no women. Practically no women, that is, and those few mostly native señoritas chaperoned by the jealous dons, or scraggly pioneer wives.

The law of supply and demand operated as rapidly in this area as it did in the matter of gambling and drinking. Within a few months, and increasingly in the first few years, the women came streaming in. The great majority of these first women were adventuresses, female Argonauts, having many of the characteristics of their male counterparts: seeking excitement, craving easy money, wanting to cut themselves a big slice of the golden pie. Some of them left by request of their governments—France and Australia, particularly. Some of them indentured their services as a means of earning passage money and woke up to find that service was to be given in the dives and fandango cellars of San Francisco. By 1851–52, women were no longer notably scarce except in the higher mountain camps. But respectable women, though they also were arriving in increasing numbers, were still a scarcity item.

When he who came to see the elephant stepped out for the first time upon the swampy avenues of San Francisco, he found himself swept up in a masquerade. Everywhere he saw flannel shirts and hip boots, black silk hats and frock coats, the satin jackets and pantaloons of the Orientals and the exotic garb of Malayans, Kanakas, native Californians and Turks. All the fancy-dress costumes of the world were assembled on these steep and perilous thoroughfares.

But rare, very rare, was that favorite sidewalk vision: hoop skirt and parasol. And nonexistent were the diversions she stood for: the ice cream socials and spelling bees, the cotillions and Sunday promenades and church picnics.

The forty-niner was of two minds about this great lack in his life. He was lonesome for his shawled and crinolined creature; he idealized her and sang songs about her and wrote her long letters. He made plans to bring her soon to the gold country (unless he planned soon to return), so that he would no longer have to shell out nuggets to the overworked Chinese laundryman who occasionally washed his shirts, or—more often—throw the shirt away when it was too stiff for comfort and buy a new one.

And yet he knew very well he was in on the spree of the century. He was part of the big holiday, and the holiday would be brief. One day the stag party would be over, and sunbonnet civilization would hunt him down and some female's silky brown braids would again chain him by a comfortable fireside.

So one central fact that set the tone for the forty-niner's pursuit of pleasure at the beginning of the golden era was: no women, save one kind of woman, and not enough of her.

On the other hand, the trouble with pleasure hunting at the far end of the golden era—say around 1860—was simply: women. Once again there were a fair number of respectable women—sisters, wives, mothers—in a word, social arbiters.

You can't have it both ways.

Either you have plenty of hell-raising, gambling, and shooting-iron saloon life, and nobody to darn your socks and cook your biscuits; or else you import the sock-darners and hearth-tenders, and they promptly establish promenades and drag you off to sprightly evenings at the ice cream parlor on the corner.

And thereby hangs a tale.

CHAPTER *2*

Magic-Lantern Country

The appearance of San Francisco at night, from the water, is unlike anything I ever beheld. The houses are mostly canvas, which is made transparent by the lamps within, and transforms them, in the darkness, to dwellings of solid light. Seated on the slopes of its three hills, the tents pitched among the chaparral to the very summits, it gleams like an amphitheatre of fire. Here and there shine out brilliant points, from the decoy lamps of the gaming-houses; and through the indistinct murmur of the streets comes by fits the sound of music. . . . The picture has in it something unreal and fantastic; it impresses one like the cities of the magic lantern, which a motion of the hand can build or annihilate.

—Bayard Taylor.

IN 1849 THE MAGIC-LANTERN CITY OF SAN FRANCISCO SWARMED WITH SHAGGY VICTIMS OF THE GOLD FEVER, MEN WHO RAN AROUND LIKE creatures possessed by a demon, collecting their gear for the trek into the gold country. The preceding spring, when news of the discovery had circulated around California early in 1848, a state-wide dress rehearsal of the Big Rush had drained San Francisco and other towns like a gigantic vacuum cleaner sucking from the heights of the Sierras. During that year the news crawled overland by oxen and seeped eastward by sailing vessel to a world at first incredulous, but quickly infatuated. By autumn of '48, the Argonauts were booking passage for the tedious voyage around the Horn or the shorter, riskier trip across the Isthmus. The Panama and Nicaragua routes sometimes took more time than the route around the Horn because ship companies allowed thousands of men to book passage as far as the

11

Isthmus without making any arrangements for ships to pick them up when they reached the Pacific side and carry them to San Francisco. Those who chose the wagon trek—less expensive, but guarded by threat of Indians, desert, starvation—could not start until spring cleared the track. But they dared not start too late, either, for autumn snowfall on Donner Pass set a deadline, and failure to meet that deadline was emphasized by memory of the fate of those Donners who had already left their name and their dead at that spot.

When they arrived at San Francisco, they found a curiously unreal town that fairly jumped with excitement. The very face of the town itself changed from week to week, as fires swept canvas and cardboard to cinders, and board shacks—later, brick dwellings—replaced them. Some of the buildings were forerunners of today's prefabricated houses: they were brought bodily around the Horn in sections and then assembled. Everything changed almost unrecognizably from one day to the next—everything but the prevailing boom-town atmosphere.

Confronting this sandy cove with its excrescence of buildings that struggled and grew like live things before your eyes, the incoming forty-niners saw a great inland bay filling up so rapidly with masts that shortly it resembled a forest. Ships were left stranded in great numbers as sailors deserted to become gold diggers. Vessels that lay nearest the shore became landlocked with the earth that laborers dumped into the shallows of the bay, filling in around the wharves, building the city out into the bay itself.

The men who arrived in '49—men who later set themselves up as the most exclusive of aristocracies on this count alone—came variously prepared for the big lottery in the hills. Some brought with them nothing but the strength in their hands and their backs. Others packed complicated Yankee machines for harvesting the gold that (according to rumor) tumbled radiant in every stream. All brought fantastic hopes and expectations. The harvesting gadgets were later used to pave the muddy streets of San Francisco, streets where mules and drunken pedestrians were jokingly said to have sunk without a trace. Iron cookstoves and casks of spoiled provisions—sometimes even sacks of flour, when flour was for a time the only cheap item of food in California—were also dumped into the quagmire until a man could proceed in comparative safety by jumping from barrel to cask to packing crate. Less visibly but just as inexorably the fantastic hopes were dumped into the swamp along with the fantastic gadgets.

San Francisco was the golden gateway. From there, men took the steamboat to one of the twin depots of the interior. Sacramento was the send-off spot for the northern mines—Marysville, Hangtown, Nevada City; Stockton for the southern mines on the Stanislaus and Tuolumne rivers, of which Sonora was the center. Men traveled by waterways as far as they could and then debarked into the interior by stage, on foot, on muleback, according to their means.

These cities—San Francisco, Sacramento, and Stockton—operated like valves in a great pump. They filled and they emptied constantly, and the people in the streets this week were not the same people you saw there last week. They looked the same, but they looked so only because they were mixed by the same recipe, with a new batch of the same ingredients: Frenchmen, Kanakas, Australians, Chileños, Yankees, Southerners, gamblers—differently costumed but identified by a common badge, that mad light in their eyes.

The fuel which kept that mad light burning—the urge for excitement and adventure that was strong as lust or hunger—carried most of these men over superhuman obstacles and into the dragging drudgery of inhumanly hard work. It lasted variously in different individuals. Some of the emigrants took their licking very soon, early enough that they met the incoming gold hunters on the trails and in the streets of Sacramento and made the best of their bad bargain by selling the newcomers their used equipment at robbery rates. Many of them confronted the upstream contingent with the bitterness of the cheated: they had seen the elephant, and found him nothing but a miserly mean jackal that ate men's souls. This warning had no effect on the horde of adventurers.

But while some were discouraged early, some became habituated to prospecting as a way of life and continued through later years chasing the phantom from one new strike to the next.

The vast majority belonged in neither class. Most of them worked in the mines for a few years and then either returned, with or without their pile, or settled down to a comparatively ordinary life in California. They sent for their families, or married in the state, and became farmers or tradesmen. A few—but surprisingly few—wrestled a fortune or the nest egg of a future fortune out of their evasive mistress, El Dorado.

After the brief pause in San Francisco to get stocked up and equipped, the average forty-niner wedged himself into cramped quarters on one of the river boats and stepped off the next morning at Sacramento. One of them (Yankee trader Franklin Buck) summed up that city in October, 1849:

> You have no idea how this country is going ahead. Last spring there was nobody here and now the people are as thick as in the city of New York. Stages run regularly to the mines; steamboats run on the rivers; a theatre, church and several large handsome hotels with billiard saloons and bowling alleys and all the fixings, have been put up. Even a couple of girls are around with a hand organ and tambourine. Civilization is making rapid strides.

When Buck refers to fine hotels, he speaks like the traditional California booster. The first hotel—the City Hotel, whose opening

14

was announced with cannon and celebrated with a five thousand dollar feast—was a wooden building costing an estimated fifty thousand to build and furnish, a showy building "clothed in a gaudy suit of flaring paints, and with a large projecting verandah and balcony." In its provision for its guests, the main emphasis was on eating, drinking and gambling. Sleep being less important, the dormitory requirement was supplied by a number of tiny cubicles and a large bunkhouse room with four tiers of bunks all around. In the center of this room was a dressing table, and above it a mirror. The hairbrush for common use was chained to the mirror-rack so it wouldn't be stolen, but the toothbrush (which each man used in turn while he waited a chance at the washbasin) was left free because nobody would bother to take it.

A woman who owned a part interest in a less elaborate hotel described a long dim room used for bar and gambling quarters as well as bunkhouse needs. Here, while one man played "Money Musk" on a cracked fiddle, another read a letter from home by candlelight, crying as he read; some lay sick in their bunks, some asleep, and out of one bunk stared down upon the dancers and card players the white masklike face of a corpse nobody had bothered to cover.

Having sampled the civilization of bustling Sacramento—a small competing copy of San Francisco—the forty-niner took the stage (if he had no mule to ride) for the high heartland of the great rush. Up into Marysville, up into Hangtown, up along the steep narrow canyons of the Yuba and the Feather rivers and their many forks he climbed, hunting free territory where nobody had yet staked a claim. Here still the magic-lantern touch persisted, and the brush and tent villages mushroomed like some kind of monstrous overnight cabbage. As most towns of "the diggings" were forced by the nature of the country to locate in canyons, the middle of town was along the edge of the creek. Up the steep canyonsides from this single road straggled the tents, the brush houses, the more permanent huts and shacks thrown

15

together from logs and boards and cloth, chinked with mud from the river. From these small centers of common living, the prospectors fanned out, up and down the rivers, staking their claims, getting down to the real business of the day.

Here they began to see the elephant in earnest. Most of them had to work many times harder than they had ever worked at regular jobs in the East, and for many the take-home pay was less. Day after day the miner stood up to his waist in icy water, torturing the muscles of his arms with the steady shaking of the broad flat pan that separated gold dust from sand. Or in the dry placer diggings of Hangtown he wielded pick and shovel while the California sun seared his naked back. At the end of the day he checked over his gains and recorded in his diary: three dollars' worth, or five, or eight. But the reason he continued and endured was that only last week the man two claims down the river suddenly struck a pocketful of nuggets and took out five thousand dollars in a day. (And why shouldn't he, another day?) The fairly lucky miner, the one who staked out on the rich diggings first, might average three to five hundred dollars a day for a short time. The unlucky ones couldn't even make expenses. But every one of them thought in terms of the man who held the winning ticket—the man who struck it rich—the man who turned overnight into a king worth thousands of dollars.

They preferred not to think of the partner who lay sick of dysentery in his cabin, or the friend from home whose leg was injured by a falling branch and who, after suffering amputation at the hands of an amateur surgeon, died of the wound. The price of the lottery ticket, like the possible prize, could not be foretold in advance when you went to the ticket window. It ranged from aching muscles to loss of life. The forty-niner was a man ready to pay the asking price, whatever it turned out to be.

16

Part of the asking price—and, oddly enough, a nuisance most of the miners complained about more than danger and illness—was the necessity of cooking their own suppers and doing their own washing. Sometimes partners cooked together, and sometimes several men bunking in one cabin assigned one of their number each day to kitchen duty. Sailors were particularly in demand, as many of them already knew how to cook. Beans and bacon were staple diet, and many a man learned how to make his own biscuits for Sundays, though pancakes were the mainstay. Vegetables were almost unobtainable (one onion cost a dollar), a fact which added scurvy to the list of occupational ailments.

As for shirts, most men wore them until they would no longer bend and then bought new ones in the cities, casting the old into the street beside the shop door. Those who were forced to rub the stiff cloth against a stone in the icy creek longed for their women and appreciated for the first time the toilsome lot of the nineteenth century housewife. One miner wrote that on Sunday—the regular washday— he and his friend went to the river to do the laundry, a task which was new to him.

> I commenced on a pair of white merino drawers which I sometimes used instead of pantaloons; they looked very well when I commenced, but [after working on them half an hour] it would have troubled an experienced washerwoman to tell what color they ought to be; I first tried soap, then sand, but it was of no use; it appeared only to *set the color*. I put them in the river and put a stone on them; what effect the rainy season had on them, I have not been able to learn.

This was a hard price to pay for freedom from feminine nagging and the chance to forget about shaving and clean collars. Many of

17

these men were like adolescent runaways: the desire to escape from home was an arrow flying west, but it was tied to another arrow flying east, the close bond most of them had with families they had never before left—and they were pulled between the arrows.

That emotional factors contributed to the breakdown of many forty-niners, a physician of the time recognized long before the days of psychosomatic medicine. Dr. J. D. Stillman wrote of Sacramento in the rainy winter of '49:

> The people at home can have no conception of the amount of suffering in the vicinity of this city. Hundreds are encamped in tents, through the rains and storms, scantily supplied with food and covering. Men are driven from the mines for want of food, and are begging for employment, asking only subsistence. Yesterday there were twenty-five deaths. The sickness does not arise from the severity of the climate but largely from overwork, scanty and bad food, disappointment and homesickness.

As the first interminable rainy winter set in, the elephant really began to stampede. Until then, the hardships of the treasure hunt had been offset by the excitement of momentarily expecting a big strike. But when the baking summer sun gave way to constant torrents of rain, the miners were driven downhill to Sacramento and San Francisco if they could afford it and dared desert their claims. Those who refused to hibernate in comparative civilization and insisted upon protecting cabin and claim with their physical presence were driven indoors for weeks at a time, and indoors in a mining camp was a very poor place to be.

If you take a husky seven-year-old boy, promise him a front seat at the biggest show on earth, and then confine him in a small room with several other boys similarly conditioned, what happens? Any

18

mother can answer that. In a sense, this was the position of the remaining miners when the rains came. But these were not seven-year-old boys, at least not on the outside. These were mostly men in their twenties possessed of great vigor and physical energy, drawn into the mountains and held there by an inconceivable excitement, holed up now with other men, whiskey and an unthinkable boredom. Everyone traveled armed as a matter of course, and almost everyone joined in the general drinking and gambling. That men were shot and stabbed regularly is no surprise; the surprise lies in the fact that mass mayhem did not result.

Being soaked to the skin much of the time didn't help anyone's temper. Some of the miners claimed that the rain fell faster inside the cabins than it did outside. One man reported he got some relief from the water leaking through the muslin roof by sleeping in a rubber cap, raincoat, and boots, with an umbrella propped over his head. "On rising in the morning," he added, "the bottle was our first consolation." Wrapped in dripping blankets, they would sit around a fire of brush, holding pieces of pork on sticks over the smoldering unwilling flame, or stirring flour and water together in a frying pan, and passing the bottle while they waited for breakfast.

After finishing this limp meal, they had a long day ahead to use up somehow. While they were working, however hard the work, they had only the evenings and Sundays to kill. Now they had to make the cards, the whiskey, the tobacco and the stories last all day long.

Those who were better educated, and who therefore missed reading matter the most sorely (one claimed later that having nothing to read was the worst deprivation of all), suffered not only the boredom of circumstance, but a chafing irritation with their low-brow comrades. William Kelly remarked bitterly that "the yawning miner . . . devoid of mental resources, turned to the indulgence of degrading appetites and propensities as a cure for *ennui.*" These high-brows had sufficient mental resources to keep themselves amused—they wrote letters and kept voluminous diaries—but too often their self-communings were interrupted by the degrading activities going on all around. The more mentionable of these are listed by Kelly as gambling, drinking to excess, which gave rise to "disgusting debauchery" not further specified, and a rivalry to see who could "narrate the most abominable story with the most obscene effect."

Except in terms of bitter complaint, the story of home amusements did not get into the record to any great extent. If you were a sojourner in a strange romantic place, what would you write home about? Would you write about evenings spent washing your socks, playing a quiet game of whist, writing the log of the day's gain if weather permitted work, while you sat up late giving the next day's beans a stir? Or would you write about your latest night on the town?

The quiet life wasn't news. The *Golden Era* wasn't interested in publishing accounts of it. The partner you left behind—that man who was too timid to join you—wouldn't be impressed or envious if you wrote of your joy in discovering a copy of one of those "yellow-kivered" trashy books—your first book in six weeks. He could go down to the library any time; writing such trivialities wouldn't make him sorry he missed out on your big adventure. So you wrote about the girls at the fandango house, even if high water had prevented your getting there for longer than you cared to think, or the boys over on the next creek who recently shot up a gambling saloon. But for the average winter-bound miner, such diversions took up far less time than talking, whittling, singing, and playing poker with cabinmates. A miner less irritated than the critic of "debauchery" turned in a more favorable report on conversational subjects: "The fate of the next

President and all presidents, the War, our 'noble selves,' " and home —always home, of course.

One evening the stories were interrupted by a sound of stealthy footsteps close by. Every man jumped to his feet, his hand on his holster. Before anyone could fire, two Mexican girls slipped into the circle of firelight. They claimed they had come to give the blond invaders a serenade, which they accordingly did, accompanying their exotic songs on guitars. After the singing came the fandango: strenuous dancing with pine needles for a dance floor and the campfire for chandelier. This is all the grateful diarist records, except to add that, when the girls left, nuggets and gold dust rattled into their outstretched tambourines.

Much more common than such incidents was the sad refrain in the diaries: "Saturday night and no place to go a courting—God bless the ladies. . . . Would that they were here in the mines by scores. . . ."

In the light of such complaints, it is puzzling to read on the next page that the same miner "Danced cotillions till after midnight." The answer is that certain of the miners, the ones with patches on their pants, were designated "ladies" for the purpose of the cotillion. One has to admire the energy of men who would pan gold in the river all day, and in the evening crave fun enough to hold a "fandango" where there was nobody to dance with but other miners.

Sometimes they broke the monotony by shooting game. This also served the purpose of adding to a sagging larder. One party of five miners went hunting in rather ponderous style, with a wagon, two fiddlers, one fiddle and a five-gallon keg of whiskey to help them endure a week's hunt through the January snow. They bagged ducks, geese, two eagles, and quite a few "jack ass rabbits," but nothing

21

which would prove really filling when barbecued. Perhaps the deer couldn't bear frontier fiddling.

Music making was a staple time killer for those who could make it, and almost a man-killer for those who had to listen. One raw gushing evening a prospector resorted to his cherished army bugle, which produced sounds that his campmates thought "would be certain death to any cow of advanced age in the *Ould Country*." The bugler was shortly challenged by a "canine amateur . . . who silenced his opponent with a few quavers and retired amidst torrents and applause." Every time the bugler tried again, the hound was ready and eventually howled his human opponent down to permanent defeat.

> Pard struck a bargain with me, [admitted young Alfred Jackson.] If I would agree not to practice on the banjo when he was around—I don't see why he don't like it for I can already play "Old Bob Ridley" and "Camptown Girls" pretty well—he would read aloud to me a new novel that he had bought: "Nicholas Nickleby," by an Englishman named Dickens.

Banjos, bugles and battered fiddles—never referred to as violins or treated as such—were the principal instruments. Sometimes it seemed that all one's friends in the amateur music line had trailed one into the mines. Those who didn't pretend to skill with any instrument at least thought they could sing, and did. Whether enduring the long evenings at home, or rocking the cradle in a pit half-full of water, the forty-niner was a great boy for a song.

"Here some Kentuckian in dulcet tones would troll you '*Old Dan Tucker*,' or one of Jim Crow's melodies," reminisced a pioneer. "Then a Cockney caroling, '*I vish I vas, and I know vhere.*' The Dutchman yonder, solacing himself with '*St. Nic'laus, goed heilig man*,' or if that was not fast enough, '*Ik ben leiderlicht*.' Monsieur, alongside of him,

22

roaring the *'Carmagnolle.'* " Sailors bellowed chanties, "Oh Santy Ana," songs of pirates, or the familiar tune of Fisher's hornpipe to words that went:

> Did you ever see the Devil
> Shovel gravel, shovel gravel,
> With a wooden iron shovel,
> And an iron wooden ladle?

A typical singing evening started with Scotch airs: "Bonnie Doon," "Highland Mary," and the "Auld Wife of Alder Valley." Then homesickness lay too heavy in the air. Somebody swore the songs were too solemn and started up a jig-time ballad that went:

> Did you ever see a gin sling made out of brandy?
> Johnny am a lingo lay.
> Did you ever see a yaller gal suckin' lasses candy?
> Johnny am a lingo lay.

The soil was right for the growth of folk songs: a group of home-sick men with common purpose and experiences, spare time, imagination, and no women around to make fun of them. Of those still extant, some, like "Hangtown Gals," are remembered because of their connection with actual or legendary events. The girls of Hangtown (Placerville) were imperious, haughty duchesses; being so scarce, they had been badly spoiled by too much masculine attention. The miners who spoiled them thought it over in their lonely cabins and commented with sour-grapes scorn:

> Hangtown gals are curious creatures,
> Think they'll marry pious preachers;
> Heads thrown back to show their features—
> Hah hah hah! Hangtown Gals.

23

"Sweet Betsey from Pike," ballads about the depredations of Joaquin Murietta, the California version of "O Susanna," original songs from Doctor Robinson's variety shows, were among the homemade items in the forty-niner's repertoire. Most are deservedly lost, and those which are left are low-grade ore, musically speaking; but they served the purpose they were meant to serve. The miner didn't care about Art, he merely wanted to amuse himself.

A circumstance that limited his choice of amusements at home in the diggings was, of course, equipment. A voice, of some sort or other, he had always with him. Cards he also had always with him—his own deck of cards, preserved with anxious care in its special case and referred to as the "California prayer book." When he opened his prayer book, the games he and his friends chose for a quiet evening were usually euchre, poker, seven-up or, among the most sedate, whist. He was about as honest as the average private in an army-camp poker game (a creature he resembled in many other ways also), but he was in sad trouble if he got caught with a pile of stolen aces in his lap. A big difference between his situation and the situation of the army private is that there were no military police around to keep his irritated opponent from shooting him. This fact helped hold the morals of card playing (or at least the skill in escaping detection) up to a high level. It may have been one of the factors in establishing the legend of the forty-niner's strict sense of personal honesty.

In the larger camps, other games were provided: billiards, bowling, foot races, an occasional game of ball. When ordinary billiards grew dull, the miner had a characteristic innovation: instead of hitting the balls with a cue, you shot them with a pistol.

If sometimes they behaved like children themselves, still many of them were fathers with children of their own at home. Missing the children (and the annoyance of the children dimmed by distance and

24

homesickness), they developed a great vogue for pets. Any man who owned a dog was considered extremely lucky. Dogs and mules were part of the family; a miner's attachment to his dog was far more intense than the average dog-lover's. The forty-niners numbered among themselves not only those who missed the babies and puppies of home, but also many misanthropes who came West because they hated society and preferred the company of dogs to that of men. In one of the saddest anecdotes of the time, a prospector records how he and his friends got stranded far from their cabin, in the winter, with snow all around and no food. They could find no game and gradually grew too weak to look for it any longer. But this man had brought his dog along. He understood that there was only one way the party could be saved, and he could not refuse, though he could not bear to watch while one of his comrades shot the dog. On the strength of their first meal in several days, the group was able to fight through the snow and back to the cabin, but the dog's owner continued to mope in the corner for a long while.

Some of them went in for pets *en masse* and vied with each other in possessing a special kind of collection. They were known to coddle squirrels, coons, wildcats and grizzly cubs. While one man boasted a domestic menagerie of one bay horse, two dogs, two sheep and two goats, another had a family circle of bobcats and mountain lions, while a third spent every spare moment building a cage for his baby bears.

Whatever the species, animals were for most pioneers a poor substitute for people. And an evening of poker in the cabin was a poor substitute for a Saturday night in town.

The abnormal, feverish craving for excitement that brought the forty-niner West in the first place was not the only factor in the wide-open gambling and saloon life of early California towns. There was also a kind of boredom—an interminable, snowbound, rained-on, half-starved, fogged-under, mindless, claustrophobic boredom—that would have driven the quietest home-lover screaming to the nearest saloon. No one who sits among his books or in front of his television set can possibly put himself in the position of the winter-bound miner in his cl th-roofed cabin, watching day after day for the rain to stop. Except for the man who remembers army life at its worst, that kind of boredom is beyond the imagination of any of us today.

No wonder the first, finest, and most important building in any town, from the tiniest canyon village to San Francisco, was the gambling hell.

CHAPTER *3*

That Howling Wilderness

"WHERE MUSIC HUSHED THE HORRID CURSE AND WOMAN TEMPTED TO PERDITION. OH THAT HOWLING WILDERNESS OF SIN AND SHAME AND crime and lust of gain. . . ."

So thundered one shocked observer when he got his first glimpse of San Francisco's Plaza, "lit by the glare of its hells." At night, the huge tents that lined the Plaza on all sides quivered and glowed like great golden balloons. Light streamed from their open doors, crossed swords of light slashing the dark teeming square. A babble of many voices shouting and cursing in many tongues rose above the background of strident banjos and drunken singing. Fortune beckoned from the bright doors. The street was muddy beneath your boots, the fog whipped in from the sea across your face, you had no home but a bunk layered between other bunks in a stinking crowded room: fortune beckoned from the blazing doorways, and you couldn't say no. Perhaps you had never gambled before in your life—but that was back East, and they didn't understand these things back East. Everyone did it here—why should you be left out?

So you walked up the path of light to the doorway, you wandered in and you watched a while, a little dazed, more than a little fascinated.

Around the roulette wheels surged the mob, crowding and pushing for a chance to fling down nuggets on the green baize table. Here

27

a white-haired, ministerial-looking gentleman dealt monte, and at the next table a lithe and wiry Frenchman called, "Faites vos jeux, messieurs," and gave you your choice of the red or the black. Over in a far corner, a dark vivid girl in Spanish dress, cigarette dangling from rouged lips, joked with the men who leaned and lurched above her. You were just off the boat; you'd never seen a señorita before. You'd never seen a woman smoke before. You had seen once, when the steamboat passed your Midwestern home, someone who looked a lot like that silent, taut-faced man in the black frock coat and skintight trousers checked in four-inch squares of green. That was a Mississippi riverboat sharper, not the kind of a man you would speak to at home. But around his table you saw dignified gentlemen, who looked like judges, pushing thin teen-aged boys aside in their eagerness to "buck the tiger."

Somewhere music was playing, strings in strange harmonies. You heard it dimly through the babble and the slap of cards on the table and the clink of glasses and bottles at the bar. The air was almost as thick as the fog in the streets outside, but it smelled different—cigars and Chinese punk, whiskey and perfume and excited people. You could not take it all in at once. Everything blended until you could no longer separate what you heard from what you smelled, what you felt from what you saw.

Through the crowd, slowly, pushing up to the table—they gave way to let you through without glancing at you—and what did you see on the table? Here was more gold and silver than you ever dreamed could exist: old greenish Spanish coins; bags and piles of gold dust; dull twisted nuggets sculptured by time and the grinding growth of the Sierra into beautiful intricate shapes. Some were round like drops of molten metal fit for a queen's earring; some were

28

warped as the gray Monterey cypress, and a few clenched in upon themselves like a warning fist or a lion's paw.

Presiding at the table, the dealer sat waiting till everyone finished placing his bet. Skillfully from hand to hand he was slipping a roll of coins, pulling out the cylindrical pile, gliding it together again, out and in like a small bellows, like a telescope, hypnotically. He snapped it down at one side and began to deal. The noise and the music went on in the background, but here right around you nobody spoke. Then the man next to you said something very quietly, and reached out his hand, and you saw a Californian winning his bet. You also saw the dealer raking in piles of nuggets and little bags of dust, but you forgot this and remembered the man beside you who won a bet, and you were lost.

When the man who came off the ship that afternoon reached deep into his pocket for a handful of coins to throw on the monte table, he was no longer a stranger. He was blood brother to the mob, no viewer of strange sights, but an actor in the scene he had recently greeted with the dazed stare of the Easterner. He had stepped into the picture.

In San Francisco of 1849, the necessities of gambling and drinking preceded the luxury of hotels and restaurants by a considerable margin. Even as late as February, 1850, half the town's dwellings were still of canvas and a third of them were saloons or gambling hells. One typical newcomer recorded: "I passed my first night in San Francisco stretched upon a form, in a tavern, where the boisterous mirth of a crude crowd of revellers effectually prevented me from dreaming of anything but drums and cymbals."

Gambling houses passed through three distinct stages. The more money and the more people in a given locality, the more rapidly they passed from one stage to the next and the more elaborate they were at

29

their zenith. In the beginning they consisted mostly of large tents, like carnival or side-show concessions. Characteristic of these was a smoky stag-party atmosphere, rough and crude, practically all male, undecorated and direct, roisterously noisy and drunk. This kind of gambling house lasted longer in the inland towns than in San Francisco, and longest of all in the mining camps.

In California's metropolis, the flood of gold, gamblers, adventuresses and Argonauts caused a forced growth of gambling establishments. They passed rapidly to the next stage. These were elaborate buildings of wood or brick, no longer serving as eating houses and all-purpose lounging rooms, but devoted solely to liquor, gambling and women. They all employed musicians and other entertainers, and in total effect achieved a high degree of big-city sophistication in an incredibly short time. These, like the tents that preceded them, were swept away in the repeating waves of flame that leveled San Francisco in '49 and '50. They were replaced with structures still more elaborate, still more dignified, still more metropolitan. They were quieter and far less crowded in this third stage. But the gambling fever was beginning to pass, and by the time the hells of San Francisco had turned into palaces, gambling was no longer the reigning passion of the country.

When one speaks of gamblers it is necessary to distinguish between "gamblers" and "men who gambled." The men who gambled included almost everyone. When anybody mentioned a gambler, however, he meant a professional. Before 1849, native Californians, disbanded soldiers and the early gold-rushees from local towns and nearby states gambled comfortably among themselves. The Spanish game of monte was universal; prospectors played chuck-a-luck (the name included all small dice games) for gold dust, played "old sledge" for drinks until they passed out, or got up a poker game with nuggets for poker chips. But gambling was almost entirely amateur.

The first steamer into the state during the spring of 1849 brought a second wave of gold seekers on the heels of the earliest forty-niners: skillful, quiet, predatory men who came West strictly for wealth, not for adventure, and who prospected far more successfully with cards than ever a man did with pick and shovel. They were expert at the profession of extracting from the pocket what the miner extracted from the claim; they and their women and the hordes of other entertainers who followed were the lucky treasure hunters, the ones who actually struck it rich in El Dorado.

They made their debut at Monterey, the first port of call for incoming ships. Here they took over the old billiard rooms, stripped the tables and converted them for use in the new games they had brought with them, set up their roulette wheels and other equipment, and started teaching the citizens the rules of "twenty-one" and "lansquenet."

One of the less businesslike of the newcomers failed to get established inside the crowded hall and had to set up his game of "sweat" under the portico, while he himself stood in his raincoat with the rain streaming upon him from the eaves.

"Step up," he called, "here's a little republican game that all can play; I ain't fancy, just a plain devil like you, if you bust I'll buy you a drink, step up, what can you lose?"

One of his listeners came forward, bet two bits, and lost.

"All right, Uncle Ned, I'm busted—gimme four bits for a drink," said he. The gambler laughed and paid up.

The real professionals wasted little time on Monterey. San Francisco was their destination. Here they turned the Plaza into a circus of gambling. The bare sandy Plaza—later Portsmouth Square—was rimmed with a continual line of gambling houses: the Verandah, the

Bella Union, "L'Aquila d'Oro," the El Dorado, Parker House and many others.

The oldest of these, the El Dorado, had grown from a tent to a three-story brick building by the autumn of 1850. Tom Maguire's Parker House, most aristocratic of the early hells, was perhaps the first American house in California. It had been brought by sailing vessel in ready-made sections and erected at once. Among the tents, this two-story wooden imitation of a country mansion was extremely impressive. After it burned to the ground, its owners rebuilt it with the added touch of marble blocks shipped 'round the Horn.

The richest claim in the Mother Lode could hardly equal one of these establishments as a money-maker. The Golden Eagle rented for fifteen hundred dollars a month when it was a canvas tent fifty feet square. The El Dorado's rent (canvas version) was forty thousand dollars a year. The Parker House rented for an annual one hundred ten thousand dollars. And they were worth it. Professional gamblers rented the tables individually, paying anything from ten dollars to one ounce gold per night for the privilege. During the high point of the gambling fever, 1849–50, the tables of the Bella Union took in as much as twenty thousand dollars in an evening. The gamblers worked in round-the-clock shifts and the doors were never closed, though of course the rush-hour crowd came between ten P.M. and dawn.

As the city expanded, the democracy of rich man and poor man, bucking the tiger in the genial promiscuity of a reeking tent, gave way to specialization. A kind of haphazard zoning developed. San Francisco became no longer one big dive, but a metropolis with business houses, homes, schools and churches growing up in the chinks between its gambling areas. The different gambling districts catered to various levels of society. Along Long Wharf, gentlemen could find "high-toned, aristocratic gambling," while over on Pacific Wharf the unwary greenhorn was likely to fall victim to "cut-throat and land-shark gamblers." Here was the riffraff of the profession, the kind of men who would relieve a miner of his pile, stun his protest with a sandbag, and shrug their shoulders if he accidentally slipped through the jagged gaps in the wharf's planking into the waters of the bay below.

Eventually there were many such districts: Chinatown; Sydney Town, rendezvous of criminals, home of the infamous Hounds; the crooked filthy alleys of Little Chile, where Mexicans and Chileños took siesta amid the garbage. From these districts you followed streets lined with taverns, tenpin alleys, "cheap-John" auction houses, stores, hotels and brothels, back to the city square. No matter how San Francisco grew, no matter what special areas developed, the heart of the city's pleasure continued to beat at the Plaza.

Here the canvas hells turned into palaces in a matter of months. Smoking lanterns were discarded in favor of ornate glass chandeliers. Their light echoed and re-echoed in wall-length mirrors. The ornate gilded roof, supported by glass pillars, added its shiny glitter to the cheap radiance of the place. Cut-glass decanters lined the shelves in back of the bar, and along it Chinese punk lay smoking in miniature junks for the convenience of cigar smokers needing a light. These were the days of red plush; rich crimson drapes hung at the long windows, and the floors were carpeted with rugs so thick that the dainty slippers of light ladies were almost lost in the rich pile.

And the wall decorations? Although the space between the mirrors was sometimes wallpapered, more often it was devoted to "licentiously seductive pictures," according to the German traveler Ida Pfeffer:

I have travelled far and wide through the world and have been among many nations who, partly from the effect of climate, and partly from the absence of religion and of education, are much given to sensual excesses; but such open and shameless enticements to evil I have never seen anywhere else, and I really believe they are only found among Christian nations and under civilized governments.

Another German traveler (foreigners were always less inhibited on paper than nineteenth century Americans) records a few details:

> The gambling halls of San Francisco give most accurate genre pictures and furnish similar examples of passionate pleasures. These gambling houses afford an impressive look into the deep chasm of ruinous passions. There are many of these buildings, which are distinguished from all others by their size, beauty and fireproofing. One comes, upon entering a large portal, directly into a richly decorated hall where the jostling crowd devote themselves to the games. . . . Adventurous figures upon sofas conveniently placed enjoy a rest in dull reflection. . . . A picture gallery arrests the attention of the onlooker and fills him with astonishment and wonder, not because of its intrinsic artistic values, but because art has been pilloried here, degraded to an agent of obscenity, offensive to morals and feelings. Most of the phases of sexual life, from the scene in paradise to that of the harem, are shown here in folio and fresco. Mythology furnished most of the subject matter, for instance, the union of Zeus, transformed into a swan, with Leda, and other similar scenes taken from the life of the gods and placed in California life.

But the murals were not exclusively devoted to glorifying the female. In a Sacramento saloon, The Plains, someone had painted his impressions of the transcontinental trek, picturing Independence Rock, Fort Laramie, and all the other landmarks. The most striking panel showed a pass in the Sierra Nevada: down the side of a clifflike mountain plodded wagon and team, seeming as if "no earthly power could prevent them from making but a single fall from the summit to the valley. These particular oxen, however, were happily independent of gravitation, and whisked their tails in the face of the zenith, as they marched slowly down."

Along with all this elegance there were dangers and discomforts other than the obvious risk of losing all your money. As the night wore on, the stale air, "impregnated with a hundred diseases, the odors of villainous rum, and the effluvia of a furnace of cigars," became more and more like a solid physical substance. And there was always the danger of being shot or stabbed, for hardly a night passed without a fight. And the structures themselves were more showy than substantial: once in a Clay Street house, while the music and roistering was at its height, the floor caved in and gamesters and gambling apparatus alike tumbled into the cellar. Everyone forgot his bruises to join in a mad scramble after rolling coins and nuggets, so the disaster was not without profit for men with quick reaction time. If this had happened in one of the dives along the wharfs built out into the Bay, it could have been a wet evening.

As you wandered from the Plaza back toward Sydney town, the elegance grew steadily less and the discomforts greater. In the wrong end of the city, you found neither the crude genial tent-saloon of the early days (and of the diggings) nor the crystal-and-plush halls of the Plaza. You found "filthy dens of vice and crime." You noted that "drunken men and women, with bloated bodies and soiled garments, crowd them at night, making the hours hideous with the bacchanalian revels." If you were a journalist, you wrote how they passed their nights in vulgar singing, dancing, quarreling, "to the music of a broken tambourine, a cracked fiddle, or a tuneless organ"—and you wrote it up with exactly this combination of frontier gusto and Puritan disgust. That was the style in which the men who patronized the dives described them for the people back home. By cultivating this attitude, they managed to cover both sides of the fence: they enjoyed at once the benefits of San Francisco's wickedness, and the moral superiority of condemning it with red-plush adjectives.

Californians were equally ambivalent in their attitudes towards the gamblers themselves. Professional gamblers were characterized in terms that range from "the aristocracy of the states" to "the black-legs that cause all our troubles." We can only suppose that, like the prostitutes they brought with them and like citizens in general, some of them were gentlemen and some of them were rascals; some of them were straight, some of them were thieving killers, and most of them were somewhere in between.

The antigambler case repeated in different words the theme expressed by Canadian William Perkins as waves of professionals swept into Sonora:

> They are the curse of this country; disreputable scoundrels who are ready for any act of atrocity. Nine tenths of the murders committed in California, up to this time, have been perpetrated by these ruffians; many of them once respectable members of the communities whence they came, but brutalized by their habits and associations in this country. They form the most blackguard and dangerous phase in the society of California.

They were also the most powerful. By infiltrating the infant political machine of the state, they were able to win positions of influence, sometimes directly but usually behind the scenes. As in other cities in later times gangsters have cracked the whip over the administration of law and order, so in this wide-open country they bribed and maneuvered their way into key spots and virtually ran the state. The

36

corruptibility of almost all legally elected officers was a considerable factor in the breakdown of official law that led to the Vigilance Committees of 1851 and 1856.

The case in the gambler's favor repeated over and over that he was openhanded and openhearted; that sometimes when he watched a young miner—fresh from the mines and ready for the trip home—start losing the stake he had saved for life in the States, he refused to allow the young man to bet any longer and put him out before he was ruined. That he was free with his money—often treating his customers to drinks on the house, the better to arouse their courage to continue playing—that he contributed lavishly to charity and supported civic enterprises, that he was the best-dressed and best-looking character in the community—all these testimonials are repeated to his credit.

In a country where wealth was the criterion of value, he had the most wealth; where generosity was honored above other virtues, he was proverbially quick with the handout. That he was so often praised by people who, at home, would have refused to meet him does not prove he was a different creature here from what he was in the conservative East. It shows, rather, that Californians reshuffled the scale of virtues, and the gambler typically possessed many of the virtues that the shuffling brought to the top.

A highly respectable woman who kept a hotel in Nevada City in 1850 had fifty or sixty gamblers boarding at her table. Writing much later, she left a picture of the gamblers she knew then, and with it an implicit picture of what California atmosphere did to soften her own attitude towards what all respectable Victorian ladies regarded as "Vice."

> Of them all I can now remember only one—Billy Briggs, who has grown to prominence in San Francisco. I see him now, portly, swarthy, and complacent, and wonder

what has become of the slender, fair-complexioned, smooth-faced, gentlemanly young man, who came and went so quietly, who carried my little boys away on his shoulders and sent them back to me happy with a handful of bright, new silver half-dollars. The "knights of the green table" were the aristocracy of the town. They were always the best-dressed men, had full pockets, lived well, were generous, respectful, and kind-hearted. They were in that day much what the stock-broking fraternity was here in San Francisco in the palmy days of the Comstock.

While the gambler was kingpin of his business, he did not operate alone. He was surrounded by the small fry: come-on girls, accomplices, musicians. He paid a barker to stand outside and drum up business; he usually kept about his table one or more "bonnets" to bet upon the right cards and win, until the suckers gawking at such luck got up sufficient courage to plunk down their gold dust. At that point the right cards stopped coming up, except once in a while to keep the customers from getting discouraged enough to go home. Very often he employed a woman—usually French, often Mexican—to deal lansquenet or monte for him, or to draw men to the roulette wheel with her eyes and her voice. The woman might be his regular mistress, or she might be earning a salary from him and picking up a little extra after hours on her own time, using her strategic position at the table to make useful acquaintances.

Mademoiselles were an increasingly common part of the gambler's retinue, and perhaps the most important lure he had. But the turnover was rapid, and he lost his bait faster than a fisherman beleaguered by a shrewd old bass. The miners took his women away as soon as they came in from France, with marriage or without, depending upon the lady's own assessment of her market value.

Another lure the gambling hells had was music. The floor shows were of questionable merit, but they were always present in some form.

They ranged from the Pike County fiddler grinding out "The Arkansas Traveler," or a wandering Italian with a barrel organ, to minstrel shows, dancers, and acts from the local theater. Shows were so often put on in the hells, and theaters were so universally accompanied by drinking and gambling annexes, that it was difficult in the early years to tell a theater from a saloon. In a Sonora dive, a pale lady in black velvet accompanied herself on the piano, singing in a husky voice the songs of Italy. The Bella Union boasted a Mexican quintette, and it was in this saloon also that the first minstrel show in California played a one-night stand, terminated abruptly when the murder of "Bones" in a brawl frightened them out of the state.

While California's infant theater struggled to get on its feet, saloons provided a temporary stage. Ventriloquists, magicians, jugglers, vocalists—every imaginable kind of act played its week or its month in the gambler's canvas palace. One ounce of gold per day was the customary wage. As time passed and the increasing population required and implemented specialization, the line was gradually drawn between theater and saloon, and also between saloon and hotel lobby, lounge, reading room.

But in the beginning, the saloon was everything. It was the forty-niner's club, it was his only recourse for meeting people outside his immediate circle, the only entertainment spot, the recreational focus of every man's life. When the forty-niner was not actually at the green tables, a great deal of his conversation revolved around what had happened there. The stories fell into two stereotypes, the choice of legend depending possibly upon the basic pessimism or optimism of the teller. In one classic, the plunger loses everything but the tattooed dancing girl on his arm; in the other, he breaks the bank. (Small moderate losing was so constant and normal that it had no stuff of storytelling in it.)

Names and details, of course, varied as the raconteur based his story on actual events. In one of the tales, a young man passing through San Francisco on his way home decided the ten thousand dollars from his claim was insufficient to cover his intended activities in the States. He went to the monte table and placed his bag of gold on the green cloth. "Will you let me stake ten thousand on one card?"

The dealer glanced at his bank, estimated his resources, and answered, "Yes."

The game of monte, which used a special forty-card deck, could be played with a layout of four cards in pairs, the bettors to place money on one pair, and the winning determined by which suit came up first as the cards were dealt. According to the rules in this story, only two cards were turned up on the table. The young man chose one and placed his heavy leather sack upon it. The bystanders deserted their play and collected to watch. The number of the card, not the suit, was to be matched.

The dealer turned over the pack. Since the bottom card did not match, he began to deal. Slowly, very slowly, he turned over card after card.

> By the Lord Harry [the observer wrote in his diary,] I should not like to have been in that young fellow's shoes! If his card is first matched, he wins; if the other, he is ruined. . . . The practiced dealer knows the under card the moment that the smallest part of its surface is exposed by the removal of the upper one. Why does he drop his hands? A general "hah" is heard as each breast is relieved from its volume of pent up air. The miner has won.

This story—probably true—was in the optimist class, so it ends with the miner anticlimatically pocketing his twenty thousand and jumping on the first ship for home. If altered by a pessimist, he would have staked the twenty thousand on the next card and lost it.

Incidents like this did happen—just as prospectors actually did strike claims which paid thousands in a day—but of course, like the pay-dirt stories they resembled, they happened with extreme rarity. Monte played honestly according to the "everything on one card" rule gave the dealer very little natural advantage. Played with the four-card layout and suit-matching rules, the bank held superior odds. But by any rules the game obviously gave an experienced sharper—a man who knew each card by the look of its back and who had incredibly nimble fingers—every opportunity to stack the deck. It is hard to believe he did not routinely do so. Cheating was an accepted part of his mores, as long as he did not get caught. Getting caught was a badge of stupidity and inefficiency, and therefore a crime, generally punished on the spot with a pistol shot.

Monte should not be confused with French monte. The latter was a skin game pure and simple, a version of the game of which-shell-covers-the-pea which gave the language its term "shell game" for all sorts of petty confidence tricks.

The Argonaut knew very well that doubling your stake or breaking the bank was a possible but highly improbable adventure. He had good reasons for gambling, but the expectation of profit wasn't one of them, though he rationalized his gambling as an attempt to increase his pile.

"Why do you do it?" a minister asked a young friend who complained of gambling losses.

"But what can I do?" the boy answered. "I didn't go in there with the idea of gambling, but to find amusement; and can you tell me what other amusement is within my reach?"

"What next, after work is done and supper finished? Sit down in that dirty ranch and think about home?" another boy demanded in-

41

dignantly of street-preacher William Taylor. "Never! I'd take the blues in an hour and be worthless for a week."

Gambling, like drinking, was at the heart of the gold-rush mood, serving alike those who would celebrate success and those who would obliterate the nagging memory of failure. It blotted out the suffocating boredom of long rainy confinement in close quarters. The kind of excitement and thrill that was the essence of gambling beat in precisely the same tempo as did the rapid pulse of the gold fever itself. It was the drug and nirvana of the treasure hunter temporarily free from apron strings, released from the weight of society's heavy hand upon his shoulder.

It is hardly strange that everyone gambled in California, that respectable people wrote apologies for gambling and found it a "necessary evil" resulting in great civic improvements because gamblers were so public spirited. (Exactly the same rationale was used later to justify the depredations of the big-time robber barons.) It was inevitable that the escapists, the gold-intoxicated, the thrill hunters made gambling their reigning pleasure and the saloon their hearth fire.

Neither was it strange that gambling as the principal pastime of a whole state could not last beyond the boom into the smash that followed. Nor could it face down the steady infiltration of civilization's fifth columnist, the respectable woman. Ten years later no man could complain—or alibi—that there was nothing to do but drink and play faro, no place to go but the shabby teeming tents and gaslit shacks of the cardsharp.

Soon the yellow bubbles that bloomed along the Plaza burst like the greater bubble of the treasure hunt itself.

CHAPTER 4

Saturday Night—and Sunday Too

THE MINER WHO "WENT TO TOWN" IN THE DAYS WHEN THAT PHRASE MEANT EXACTLY WHAT THE WORDS SAY (THOUGH THE PRECISE MEANing carried implications more glorious than it would now) could afford the luxury of a big splurge very seldom. How often he could manage it was determined by how much gold he took out of his claim, how much time he could spare, and which town he chose. If he wanted to go to the next big village, Marysville or Hangtown or Sonora, he could easily arrange it almost any Saturday night. According to his temperament and resources, he could enjoy these little constant sprees or he could save his gold for a trip to Sacramento. With a little more planning and foresight and saving, he could undertake a week's vacation in San Francisco. Most forty-niners tried to combine the advantages of both, but different individuals emphasized one more than the other. While the big guns kept their powder dry for a great rare explosion, how did the small ones pop off on Saturday nights?

Gamblers were everywhere in the diggings. The woods—if the word applies to the great dark pines of Sierra canyons—were literally full of them. Whenever a "strike" was made in the mountains and a few prospectors perched their tents under the eaves of the cliffs, the monte dealers swept down upon them and turned the newborn camp

43

into a place where "the *many* reproduce pandemonium in more than its original horror, while the few honestly and industriously commence digging for gold." In a matter of weeks, up mushroomed the more "permanent" structures, low-spreading skeletons of logs or frame with white cloth nailed over them, or shacks flung together from rough boards and lined with old newspaper.

As Sacramento and Stockton gambling hells were downgrade versions of San Francisco's palaces, so were the mountain-village saloons and the tents of the diggings imitations in decreasing order of elegance. Each was like a dimmer carbon copy of the original model. But the mining-camp "deadfall" had a flavor of its own. It was an all-purpose general store that sold liquor and had gambling tables available. Sometimes the proprietor rented a table to a professional gambler; often they were a free convenience for the use of drinking customers who rolled the dice or dealt a round of poker while they drank. The deadfall was the community center of the diggings.

As elegance varied, so also the noise, the confusion, the roistering and excitement varied—but in the opposite direction. Glass chandeliers were not nearly so likely to be shot to bits as were the smoky tallow lamps of some mountain saloon that was the only wooden building in the camp.

The saloon at Rich Bar's "Empire Hotel" was typical of the more substantial frontier dives. The hotel was a two-story board structure, roofed and fronted with canvas, and graced with the luxury of two or three glass windows. Some of the interior walls were painted in delicate pastel hues, and, if you thought this showed that woman's touch which does everything to make a house a home, you would be right. The place had originally been built for two prostitutes, but had been deserted by them when their business unaccountably failed. The gambling saloon was typically fitted with "that eter-

44

nal crimson calico . . . in the center of a fluted mass of which gleams a really elegant mirror, set off by a background of decanters, cigar-vases, and jars of brandied fruit; . . . A table covered with a green cloth—upon which lies a pack of monte-cards, a backgammon board, and a sickening pile of 'yellow-kivered' literature—with several uncomfortable-looking benches, completes the furniture of this most important portion of such a place as 'The Empire.' "

Though small in comparison with city houses, mining-town saloons like this one were big business. The house of Smith and Barker in Nevada City held fifteen faro tables, always crowded. Faro was characteristically American; those who played it "bucked the tiger." Like poker, it was more adapted to amateur play than to commercialized saloons because, if honestly played, the percentage in the dealer's favor was slim. Also it required no complicated equipment and thus was suitable for the here-today-and-gone-tomorrow saloons of the diggings. An ancient and complicated banking game, probably introduced into the United States through New Orleans from France, it was peculiarly open to cheating, since the professional had no other means of assuring himself a safe margin of winnings. It offered the bettors a thirteen-card layout. A customer placed his bet on one card. Then the cards were withdrawn in pairs from a special box just large enough to hold the pack. The face-up top card, called the "soda," did not count; the second card, placed face up next the box, was the loser. The one left face up in the box was the winner. The winner was then placed a few inches away from the box, and the dealer proceeded with the next pair. The last card left in the box, called "in hoc," was like soda a dead card, counting for no one. Thus the phrase "in hoc" came to stand for failure. Players were allowed to rearrange their bets between turns, but of course could not touch cards while the pair was being shown.

Other games were as closely identified with nationalities as poker and faro were with Americans, or monte with Mexicans and Latin Americans. The Frenchman's favorite, roulette, was unwieldy for use in the camps because it required a special table with wheel in the center and the layout painted at each end. Sometimes a game came to be associated even more narrowly with a certain town, as keno was with Placerville and monte with Sonora.

The social atmosphere of Sonora differed from that of the average mountain town because of a mixture of nationalities notable even in a time and place where every camp was full of exotic characters. It had been settled early in the rush by Mexicans and South Americans. When the Yankees came into Sonora, they were inclined to lump all the "foreigners" they found settled there under the title "greaser." Among themselves, however, the Spanish-descended peoples drew intricate class lines which rated a person's caste primarily according to the amount of Indian and Negro blood, and secondarily by skin coloring. To be dark-faced but mostly "white-blooded" was socially superior to being fair of face but possessed of the hidden black or brown tinge. Very soon French adventurers of both sexes began to pour into the state, and large numbers of them found Sonora a peculiarly congenial climate. Because of the Frenchman's skill and the Mexican's passion for gambling (his motto was, roughly and confusingly translated: "Woman for food, silver for dress ornaments, gold for monte"), Sonora was notoriously wide open in a culture where it was difficult to be notorious on this count.

Young William Perkins, who came from Canada but fell so in love with Spanish ways during his Sonora sojourn that he finished his career a naturalized Argentinian, left a portrait of Sonora early in 1849. At this time most mountain towns were just getting started, and Nevada City had not even been founded.

On Saturdays and Sundays, the old Camp used to wear, night and day, an almost magic appearance. Besides the numberless lights from the gaily decorated houses, all of them with their fronts entirely open to the streets, the streets themselves were strown with lighted tapers. Where there was an open space, a mexican would take off his variegated zarape, lay it on the ground, put a lighted wax or sperm candle at each corner and pour into the centre his 'pile.' . . . The zarape would soon be surrounded by his country-men, who, seated on the ground would stake and generally lose their hard-earned weekly wages.

It would have been difficult to have taken a horse through the crowded streets; as for wheeled carriages, they were not known yet. Tables loaded with 'dulces,' sweetmeats of every description, cooling beverages with snow from the Sierra Nevada, floating in them, cakes and dried fruits, hot meats, pies, everything in the greatest abundance. One could hardly believe in his senses, the brilliant scene appeared so unreal and fairy like. On either side of the street were ranged the gambling tables generally covered with a rich scarlet gold embroidered cloth, in the centre of which would be displayed a 'bank' of perhaps a thousand ounces, in silver dollars, gold doubloons or small bags of gold dust. Coins of both metals, commanded a premium of ten fifteen and sometimes twenty per cent for gambling purposes in these times.

The tables belonged to the different habitations outside of which they were placed.

These board huts, sometimes shacks made of poles covered with brush, were almost too flimsy to stand against a breeze, but out of the sticks and brush fluttered gay flags and tattered bits of bright cloth. Anyone who wanted to rent the table and call himself a gambler had to pay from twenty dollars to two ounces of gold per night, the rate depending on location.

Behind the tables, across the front of the open stalls, ranged a rough wooden counter, and here all kinds of liquor sold for fifty cents a glass. In drinking as in gambling, the Mexicans were insistently carefree: "it was nothing uncommon to see a Mexican enter, call for a bottle of brandy which was worth an ounce, and, taking a wine glass, deliberately pour the whole contents of the bottle into it, spilling, of course, all that the glass would not contain."

Close by the table and the hut with its board bar, and its tinsel bravado of lighted tapers and banners, Mexican bands—sometimes strings, sometimes a curious trio of clarinet, harp, and bass guitar—struck up gay fandango tunes. "The noise of drums, guitars, fiddles and the ringing metallic thrum of the little mexican lute, never for a moment ceased from Saturday to Monday." While the band played, the Mexican women, heads covered with *rebozos*, moved about in their makeshift kitchens, cooking *tortillas* and wrapping them around the mixture of meat and chile powder which was their national staple. Whenever there was room, you would find couples dancing the traditional strenuous dances from Spain and South America.

The French adventurers who settled in Sonora had definitely found their El Dorado. Their approach was characteristically shrewder and more cold-blooded than the Latin-American. Among other games, they imported the perilous game of lansquenet, exiled from Paris where authorities had banned it because it caused too many fights. This was a banking game in which the customers bet against each other—that is, a player would put up five dollars as "the bank" and another bystander would cover that amount with his own bet. Then the proprietor of the table—almost always a Frenchwoman—handed the bank maker cards mixed together from several decks. He set up two cards: one for his bank, the other for his opponent. He then dealt, the first matching card of course being the winner. If his card matched, his stake was doubled, but he had to leave it on the table. His opponent could retire while others bet against the bank (an individual or several together making up the amount) or he might continue. If the one who challenged the bank should win, he could take his money and leave. But the man who made bank in the first place had to win three times (the stake doubling each time) before he could withdraw.

The duty of mademoiselle—aside from her function in luring players there in the first place—was to act as middleman. She furnished the table and cards. She made sure everyone placed his money on the table when he bet. When the challenger lost, she—not the dealer—took his money; when he won, she handed over to him the bank that the dealer made. She was a referee. She did not deal or control the bank, as in other games. All that she got was the amount of the original stake after the bank maker had won three times. When he won, she took the bank, subtracted her percentage and handed over his winnings to him.

Because it provided a hand-to-hand encounter between amateurs, with mademoiselle merely holding stakes, lansquenet was peculiarly liable to become a focus of gunplay. This was what happened in the clash between two Sonorans named Cardwell and Ford.

Cardwell made bank at three dollars. Ford bet the whole amount, but did not lay his money on the table as the rules required him to do. Cardwell dealt and won. The bank stood at six, although Ford still had shown no money. This continued until the bank stood at twenty-four, and Cardwell, having won three times, was entitled to collect. Ford should have been putting down his gold, and Mlle. Virginie holding it. At this point she would have paid Cardwell his winnings, minus her own take—twenty-one dollars for him, three for her.

Cardwell asked Mlle. Virginie for his money. At once Ford said insolently, "You have to look to me for that money."

"I do not know you in the transaction," said Cardwell. "I look to the table for my money."

"No sir," said the other, "it is with me you have to settle and if you behave decently, I may perhaps pay you."

With more sharp words criticizing the manners and ancestry of Ford, Cardwell repeated, "The table is responsible to me. Settle you with Mlle. Virginie, as you please, but do not try and force a quarrel on me at this moment for you are armed and I am not!"

Ford did not draw his revolver—it was unpardonable to draw on an unarmed opponent—but walked silently around the table, took Cardwell by the arms and bent him back over the green baize. In the fight both fell and Ford, being on top, bit Cardwell's lower lip off. Others interceded at this point and took Cardwell off to have a surgeon patch up his face.

Half an hour later Cardwell came back with a friend, a young man named Coffman.

"Bill Ford, I am come to kill you," he said, and while Ford was drawing his gun, shot him in the chest. Cardwell and Coffman ran away with the police in pursuit. The police fired and accidentally killed Coffman, who had only come into the story as moral support for Cardwell.

Nobody blamed Cardwell, since they considered he had acted under unbearable provocation, and the usual on-the-spot jury exonerated him. Everyone was glad Ford got killed, since it saved the Vigilance Committee trouble and expense, but it was very sad that poor young Coffman had to get caught in the cross fire.

William Perkins reported that later:

> I then paid a visit to the beautiful Mlle. Virginie, whom I found calmly continuing her game as if nothing had happened. She greeted me with a fascinating smile.

"Ah Monsieur, quel horreur!" turning up her brilliant eyes towards the roof and dealing slowly the cards at the same time.

I made her describe the circumstances to me, which she did with all the calmness she would have evinced had she been relating a scene from a novel. To me, her delicate white hands seemed smeared with blood and I left in disgust. . . .

Perkins repented of his disgust very soon, however, and added:

But I am talking flat treason against our only polka partners. It won't do. We must lay aside some straight-laced ideas and accommodate ourselves as best we may, to the extraordinary scene we find ourselves actors in.

And so they did, these forty-niners. Most of them managed quite well to accommodate their strait-laced, civilized, Eastern, church-inculcated ideas to the peculiar moral climate of gold rush California.

Where families existed, East met West and neither one came out always the winner.

Hinton Helper, a cynical disparager of California who later wrote the famous *Irrepressible Conflict,* records an incident that took place at a hotel where he stayed overnight. The landlord had his family with him, including a boy named Ned who was not quite nine. After supper Ned joined the other men at the nightly card game, handling the cards as well as anyone else. A quarrel developed, and someone claimed Ned had shifted the cards. Furious with his accuser—a grown man three times his size—Ned claimed here was a "liar and a scoundrel," adding, "Goddam you, I'll shoot you." Everybody chose sides and began firing. When one of the men stopped a bullet, people instantly seized the person who fired that bullet, yelled, "Let's hang him!" and made for the nearest tree, where they hanged him.

Though he had touched off the fracas, nothing at all happened to Ned. There wasn't much left, short of hanging, that could happen to Ned. With such a head start along the primrose-and-noose road before he was nine, he probably did not linger among his gambling companions very long.

More often home won and the Wild West lost. One of the many forty-niners who wrote begging his wife to make a home for him in the diggings got his wife, all right, but then what? The first Sunday after she arrived in camp, the men as usual flung a blanket over the table as soon as she had cleared away the dinner dishes, and sat down to their customary game of monte. But Mama wouldn't have it for a minute: did they think they could gamble in *her* house on Sunday, who did they think they were? Out they went, to continue the game under a pine tree. As daylight faded, they faced the horrible thought, "game called on account of darkness." But the dealer, who was winning, paid two husky fellows fifty cents an hour each to split wood and keep up a fire. So in the mountain chill, by the leaping glare from a campfire, the banished game went on. The woman's touch might make a canvas shack a home, but it definitely altered what went on in that home. This was the moral the homesick miners who told the tale pointed out to other homesick miners, pining for their womenfolk.

In all the dives, from San Francisco to the Mother Lode country, the forty-niner talked of home and women between games. The Mexican string quintettes strummed waltzes, the fiddlers sawed out "Old Zip Coon," the trios sang, and all the cacaphonous crowd wailed together the nostalgic melodies of home.

(Home, sadly yearned for by those who reached the maudlin stage, faraway home where mother would have put the swaggering big-shot gambling man to bed with a dose of good old sulphur and molasses to purge him of his reckless, crazy foolishness.)

But homesick as he might be, the forty-niner had what he wanted. Otherwise there was nothing to stop him from going home. This way, he had the dream of home and the marvelous freedom from all the restrictions that home implied.

Home moved in on him during the years that followed. Home did not survive the encounter with the Wild West unaltered, untouched, but home did succeed in pushing gambling from its pedestaled palace into the back street dens of Chinatown, where it was no longer a whole state's pleasure, but merely one more scrap of Vice clinging to the interstices of Victorian society.

CHAPTER 5

"Drunkard's Heaven"

In short, the mines may, with some propriety, be called the gamblers' and drunkards' heaven, and to crown the scene, the Christian's Sabbath is the great day of trade and bull fighting and drunkenness and licentiousness.

WHEN MORALISTS DENOUNCED VICE IN CALIFORNIA—WHICH THEY CONSTANTLY DID IN THE JUICIEST LANGUAGE AT THEIR COMMAND— they lumped gambling, prostitution, drinking and Sabbathbreaking all together, with one hardly more serious than another. The forty-niner tended to lump these things together, too, but he regarded the resulting composite with an entirely different attitude. He would probably have replied that he did not intentionally break the Sabbath: it was just that in California Saturday nights lasted through to Monday mornings.

That the forty-niner was a drinking man—as well as a gambling man and a man with a quick trigger finger—is a primary part of the picture that has come down to us. How much of the picture was true?

We read in many an Argonaut's letter home some such message as: "Tell Mother not to worry about me. I have not broken my promise to abstain from intoxicating drinks, although all around me the advocates of the Demon Rum seem to flourish."

And then we read of a hunting expedition which carried among essential supplies a ration of about one pint of whiskey per day per man.

Journalist Frank Soulé—a yellow journalist if there ever was one

—left a sensational picture of debauchery and intoxication in his *Annals of San Francisco*. But a prospector commented in his journal, "Although drinking was universal, drunkenness was rare in the mines in those days."

In spite of comments like that and promises to Mother, most of the evidence seems to confirm the stereotype of gold rush California as a land that might well be aquatically parched in the summer and flooded in the winter, but was alcoholically extra damp all year around.

"I went into a board shanty a few yards square, where they sold liquor and had a glass of wine," wrote a pioneer named Swan. "It was the only house there, and was the beginning of Sacramento City."

A typical beginning. And when the town burned down, the quickest recovery in a land of quick recoveries was the liquor trade. After one Sacramento fire, a saloonkeeper had a canvas establishment set up before the ashes were cold and was carrying on a thriving business selling drinks to the volunteer firemen. Fire fighters were thirsty customers.

For the most part every saloon looked like its brother, but a few were somewhat distinctive. When the storeship *Apollo* was stranded far from San Francisco Bay by the filling in of the shallows, Californians quickly converted it into a tavern. Having once been seaworthy, the *Apollo* and similarly converted ships were among the sturdiest of early drinking houses. Certainly its barnacled bulkheads would take more of a beating from flying fists and stray bullets than the swarming tents of San Francisco's Happy Valley, the campground of transients en route to the mines, where canvas walls shook and bulged beneath the weight of unsteady customers until it looked as if the tents themselves were swaying with intoxication or hopping up and down in furious joy.

Nobody made a statistical survey of the drinking resources of California, but there were some estimates. Historian Hubert Howe Bancroft claimed 537 places sold liquor in San Francisco in 1853. Not all of these were exclusively bars—he counted also gambling hells, restaurants, theaters, billiard saloons and those places euphemistically referred to as "fandango cellars." Hinton Helper, observing California with prim disgust that same year, put it this way: If San Francisco allotted one saloon to every street corner (four per intersection), there would still be some left over.

> Of the two hundred and fifty thousand inhabitants in California, from twelve to fifteen thousand are exclusively engaged in this diabolical, but lucrative business; and, what is worse than all, nearly one-fourth of the bars are attended by young females, of the most dissolute and abandoned character, who use every device to entice and mislead the youthful and unsuspecting.

Having delivered himself of further diatribes on the subject of liquor and women, Helper continued with a most self-revealing comment:

> Lest we should fall in love with one of these sirens, we will not go near them, but will enter one of the saloons kept by a biped of our own sex.

Here is condensed into a sentence a typical mid-nineteenth century attitude toward gold rush culture: a kind of peeping-Tom puritanism that alternately shuddered, denounced, and peeked through its fingers with utter fascination.

While such bias must be taken into account when the same informant stated that California consumed an annual five million gallons of liquor, this estimate fits very well with the rest of the evidence.

56

In San Francisco, types of saloons ranged all the way from the gentleman's club to the dives of Sydney Town. It was not safe to stray into the latter area and get taken in by the names that hung swinging above the doors of filthy little dens: The Boar's Head, the Bird in Hand, the Jolly Waterman, the Tam O'Shanter. The names might have the flavor of genial English pubs, but the owners came straight from the penal colonies of Australia.

It was in places like these, and also in the crude, rugged deadfalls of the diggings, that incidents took place which were later molded and gilded by Hollywood writers into the stereotype of the Wild West Saloon.

> Again I met him in "shooting McGee's" saloon in Yreka [boasted the Argonaut]. I was standing at the bar in company with many others. "Study" had just poured out a big glass of brandy and I was lighting a cigar when some one crowded in beside me and called for drinks; turning, I saw it was Willy. I snatched "Study's" glass and saying some appropriate words dashed the brandy into his face. Then we "had at it" again.

And the fight was on. Our rather arch commentator doesn't tell what happened, but it was probably anticlimactic anyway. It was surprising how often people came out of these deadly "shooting affrays" nursing a cut lip or a bruised posterior. But in the stories there were usually—as often there were actually—bullet wounds and bashed heads. Thus at Shooting McGee's and in similar tents and shacks, the forty-niner enthusiastically scratched out with his bowie knife the rough outlines of the picture later generations would see whenever his name was mentioned.

Men like the writer of this account had apparently already digested the popular image of the Argonaut and made it their self-image. They were quick to throw brandy glasses around when the honor of

57

the clan required such behavior, even though they would probably have acted otherwise at home. And they recorded their exploits with bravado. It is impossible to say how much of this behavior, in drinking and in general brawling, was determined by spontaneous motives and how much by a romantic picture of the Wild West that was already taking an ineradicable grip upon the minds of men.

Miners on a spree were often far less dangerous than they and their audience liked to think. All the boys would get together and advance upon the local deadfall. Here they would pour Monongahela whiskey—the popular drink of the frontiersman—down their throats all day long. Evening came, and somebody proposed going home. Several men agreed, but others said no, so they settled this by having another round. Then someone claimed that so-and-so had failed to treat the company. He acknowledged the fault and ordered one more for everybody. Somebody else thought of mutual friends at home—naturally everyone had to toast these friends. Joe Price proposed they should go all together the next day to the dry diggings in a neighboring gulch and prospect for better claims. All in favor of going with Price tomorrow, on this side of the room; opposed on the other. Opposed were in the minority, they had to treat. At this some boys lost their temper and started for their tents: some went up the mountain and some went down, and some went into the creek. Of the twenty men who enjoyed this particular party, not one got back to his own tent. But not one got stabbed or shot, or even drowned.

This was a far more typical bender than the traditional brawl, stabbing, and "shooting affray."

Accounts of alcoholism written in dirge tempo were usually turned out either by temperance people or by participants remembering their sins in their old age and drawing a moral for the benefit of the young. The miners themselves took the hazards of Demon Rum rather lightly. Alfred Jackson wrote about a neighbor named Andy Collins who was a hard drinker:

> He bought his rum by the gallon and kept soaked all the time. Tuesday night he had a bad attack of the jim-jams, and his nearest neighbor, O'Neil, heard him yelling and shrieking like all possessed. He rushed down, opened the door and found Collins cowering in one corner, striking at imaginary swarms of imps in the air. "Don't you see them?" he yelled; "little devils with tin jackets on. Look at them coming down the chimney and through the window, hundreds of 'em!" With that he rushed through the door, out into the rain and darkness, and O'Neil lost sight of him.

O'Neil roused the camp and everybody formed a posse to reclaim their erring brother. But neither the boys nor the tin-jacketed imps caught up with Collins; cold and exposure nearly did. They found him some time later, carried him home and nursed him back to health.

Sometimes a couple of individuals with extra strong stomachs competed to see who could hold the most. Wrote William Kelly:

> I was induced . . . to look on at a Yankee drinking match, perfectly in character. . . . It took place at one of the open booths on the [race] course, attracting a great crowd and giving rise to fresh bettings. The man who won the toss for choice of fluids selected port wine, each tumbler having a raw egg broken into it—a potion that appeared to take his opponent by surprise; however, they went to work, and, with the short necessary pauses, got up as high as the ninth glass each, when one betrayed symptoms of distress.

This poor devil got sick on his tenth, but the winner went on to drink number thirteen, and then in a spirit of bravado drank his spectators' health in a bumper of brandy and water.

While brandy and whiskey were the staple liquors of the Argonaut (as of frontiersmen in general), they were only two items on a staggering list of possible drinks. The whiskey supply could not catch up with the gold-hunter's mammoth thirst, and he had to accept substitutes: rum, gin, even—if his taste ran to lighter refreshments— ale, porter, cider, claret, port, Barsac and hock. No urban party was a party without champagne. For those with delicate palates and a sweet tooth, there were peppermint cordials, cherry cordials, and similar liqueurs. Increasing sophistication brought the fancier mixed drinks: sherry cobblers, mint juleps, rum punches, brandy smashes, and mixtures with peculiar names that were ancestors of modern cocktails and highballs. The problem of iced drinks was solved, at least in the mining towns, by the widespread use of snow brought in on muleback from the mountain tops. Winter holidays called for the same eggnogs and the hot potables that people drink today.

Liquor served many purposes then as now. No business could be carried on in California cities without a drink to make it legal. Any good saloon probably saw more important transactions consummated than did the plushiest office of San Francisco's financial center, Montgomery Street. A drink was the accepted way of greeting an old acquaintance, cementing a new friendship, reconciling a quarrel, solidifying a deal with a new mademoiselle just off the boat. Naturally decent women were never seen in saloons in those days, but they were seldom seen anywhere in 1849–50.

However, in the liquor trade, as in other kinds of merchandising, the supply-and-demand problem proved tricky because of slow communications between California and the States. When at first there was a shortage of liquor, dealers wrote home for huge quantities. These arrived, and prices fell. Fifty cents a glass was the cost for a drink in the beginning; very shortly it was twenty-five cents. In 1853 W. W. Haney, who had kept the bar in the American Theater, opened the Golden Gate Saloon on the "bit" plan. (The "bit" was an actual coin worth twelve-and-a-half cents.) As an additional lure, the Golden Gate provided a free reading room where customers could scan the latest newspapers and wrangle over politics. This, the five-and-ten of the saloons, was looked upon with considerable bitterness by bar owners who still charged the usual two bits per drink.

Early in the fifties the crowded and competing saloons of San Francisco offered the additional enticement of the free lunch. This institution began humbly in the form of crackers and cheese, or anything salty to increase the customer's thirst. But rivalry developed the simple fare into a full-blown dinner of soup, fish, roast meat and side dishes. In 1851 the Pacific Exchange advertised an eleven o'clock meal of "hot lamb and beef stew, soused salmon, Neufstadt anchovies, lobster salad, pickled beets, cucumbers, crackers, butter, cheese and bread." This "lunch" was topped off with a Boston Ice. To get it, you bought a drink. And in 1851 food prices were still inflated, though you no longer paid a dollar for an onion or an egg.

Inevitably the free lunch became the Frankenstein's monster of the California saloon. A tavern had to furnish lunch or lose its customers to one that did. But if it joined in the scramble to beat everybody else in this way, food prices quickly drove it into bankruptcy. By 1853 gold no longer flowed as freely as it had in '49 and '50; the bubble of the gold rush was showing thin places, warning of its eventual bursting. Hundreds of loafers were swarming into the saloons until by the mid-fifties one writer estimated that five thousand people, nearly ten percent of San Francisco's population, would have starved without the free banquet in the taverns.

Caught in this trap, the saloonkeepers fell back on psychology and advertising. In 1853 the newspaper advertisement of the Headquarters Saloon appealed to everyone's snobbery and higher instincts:

61

We go in for the "nimble shilling," and, to make it pay, must reduce the general expense usually attending a first-class saloon. We have done so in one great *item*. *We set no Lunch*, and a gentleman can call in and refresh himself with a fine glass of "Duff Gordon" Sherry, an extra glass of clear old English Ale or Porter, or, if he prefers, as good a Poney or Punch, Cobbler or Cocktail, as can be produced in town, without the necessity of calling up a half dozen or so of hungry *boarders*.

The liquor habits of Californians, with or without free lunch, drew to that state eager missionaries of the various temperance societies. Their success increased as hard times shook the state. Although poverty had driven many men to the free lunch, it had the opposite effect on numerous others, and drinkers without the price of a drink would listen to those who demanded they remember their eternal souls. Sometimes the missionaries converted a whole town at once, and the people took the pledge en masse. This might be due to the evangelist's zeal, but more often to the sobering effects of some recent tragedy due to drunkenness. As a total population habit change, however, it rarely outlasted the missionary's visit to the town. In 1853 the people of Mokelumne Hill took half the temperance pledge: they promised to consume nothing stronger than lager beer. In evidence of good faith, the villagers drank a hundred and twenty gallons of beer that Sunday evening.

Another evidence of increasing tameness in the mines was reported by an Englishman: "What struck me most as a sign of civilization, was seeing a drunken man, who was kicking up a row in the street, deliberately collared and walked off to the lock-up by a policeman. I never saw such a thing before in the mines." In fact, at first he was almost shocked to see the police infringe upon what he had come to accept as man's natural right to get drunk as a pig and roll in the gutter.

Civilization got to San Francisco a bit more rapidly. In July, 1851, out of two hundred and fifty crimes brought to court, seventy-two were "drunk and disorderly." Many cases were women. Policemen used to go their rounds with handcarts, fishing disheveled ladies out of the street and carting them off when they were unable to stay on their feet.

In general, however, police didn't cause too much trouble to convivial spirits who drowned their sorrows and celebrated the glories of the rush in California's teeming saloons. They had a great deal to forget and a great deal to celebrate, and the law, adapting to the spirit of the times, was lenient and relaxed.

CHAPTER *6*

Sunbonnet, Rebozo, and Harlequin Masque

I may not be a competent judge, but this much I will say, that I have seen purer liquors, better segars, finer tobacco, truer guns and pistols, larger dirks and bowie knives, and prettier courtezans here, than in any other place I have ever visited; and it is my unbiased opinion that California can and does furnish the best bad things that are obtainable in America.

—Hinton Helper.

Hating California, Hinton Helper was nevertheless forced into paying tribute in a style typical of the "viewers with alarm." Unfortunately, it is only from those who felt it was their moral duty to denounce Sin that one can get information about some of these best bad things, including the best bad women.

When the curious reader digs up a mass of journals, letters and other contemporary records and attempts to pan out of this rocky jumble the shining dust of truth about men and their women, he finds he is working very low-grade ore. Yet there is no use prospecting for a better claim. Men did not often leave this kind of gold lying around loose for the eyes of the inquisitive. There were some things you could not put in a letter to Mama in Massachusetts, and you could not always be sure even your diary was safe from prying. Besides, sex itself was the unmentionable, the unprintable.

Yet the dust filtered in anyway, between the lines. It could not.

be kept out, even by the inhibitions of the day, when the idea of woman was necessarily so obsessive to wifeless men.

First one must understand that when women are mentioned by those who left us their notes on the subject, the writers did not necessarily mean "all members of the female sex." The writer could take for granted his reader's knowledge that there were only two kinds of women. Depending upon the fact that this was God-given truth, universally accepted, the contemporary writer confuses later readers by sometimes omitting the words "respectable" or "fallen"; these words are tacitly understood and must be gained from context. The American man coming into California in the fifties brought with him a ready-made idea of woman inculcated by the moral climate of the mid-century United States. He did not know, acknowledge, or even consider that there could be any females who did not fit into one of his two categories. The concept was absolute: woman was virtuous or she was disreputable. She could be nothing in between.

Which class she belonged to depended upon one circumstance: her sexual chastity, or her lack of it. The maiden and the wife were sacred; the woman who transgressed—and was caught—found herself picked up by force of custom, as a chess player picks up a pawn, and moved in her entirety over to the wrong side of the board. Nothing she did ever after, as an individual, altered her classification. She could no more re-enter the caste of the blessed (though as a Magdalene figure, she could win forgiveness) than an Englishman could enter the ranks of Brahmins.

Once this is understood, the confusion in the record disappears. You read the flat statement: "There were no women in the mines then"; but you have just seen an account of girls dealing monte in the next town, or the story of a fandango where women were present. These statements do not contradict each other; they merely seem to do so because the man who wrote "there are no women here" left tacit the qualifying word "respectable."

Nevertheless in the spring of 1849, and much later in the more remote mountain villages, women of either kind were scarce. Generalization is made more difficult by the fact that presence or absence of women, and balance between the two recognized classes, varied sharply from one month to the next and from one town to its neighbor.

A few women—the sunbonnet women, the true pioneer mothers—came across the plains with their husbands in the very beginning. The number of these grew steadily, and their ranks were increased in the early fifties by the constant arrival via sailing vessels of wives who had been sent for by their husbands. But in 1849 they were so comparatively few, even in the cities and particularly in the gold towns, that they had no appreciable effect upon the constant complaints of "no women in California." In fact their occasional presence, reminding everyone of the contrast between California and home, only served to exaggerate their scarcity and call forth elaborate demonstrations of homesickness and chivalry.

Many stories grew up about this lack of good women. The universal anecdote related how a group of miners stumbled upon a piece of a lady's hat. With great joy and generosity, they sent out invitations to a grand ball. Three hundred miners gathered round on the appointed day, each dressed in a red flannel shirt and bringing a bottle of brandy. The reception committee drove a stake into the ground at the exact spot where the hat was discovered, placed the hat on top of the spike and draped a blanket around to represent the female form. Beside it they placed a miner's cradle with a smoked ham in it. After each dance the chairman of the meeting rocked the cradle, while the secretary poured brandy down the back of the lady's neck. The ball went on for two days; at the end of that time they surveyed the territory of their totem fandango and called the town Auburn. This is undoubtedly apocryphal.

One forty-niner related how he discovered the print of a woman's slipper in the mud; how he followed the print for miles and came finally upon a camp, which he did not dare approach very closely. But peering through the shrubbery, he could see protruding from beneath the edge of the tent that very pair of slippers, with feet in them. However, there were great crude boots in the vicinity, also containing feet, and the miner wistfully withdrew without attempting any exchange of greetings.

The attitudes shown in these stories run like a constant thread through all accounts of the earliest times. An occasional woman-hater raised a note of cynical dissent. When Alfred Jackson was sitting by his cabin in the evening enjoying "the wind singing through the pine trees, the frogs croaking in the creek," and reflecting "only one thing was wanted to make it perfect—a good woman for a companion to enjoy it with you," his partner answered, "You remember what happened when Eve came into Paradise? She would make you move into town, put on store clothes and wear a collar. You could not get her to sit out under the tree for fear of snakes." Then he laughed and said: "Make the most of it—it won't last forever."

That was a smart man. But the attitude of worshipful homesickness for woman persisted, and there must have been considerable reason for it, especially in the mines, where lack of women continued to be a dominating theme for some years. Even in San Francisco there was a brief period when men would trail a woman along the streets just to enjoy the sight of her. The women who received this attention were startled at first, but came to accept and enjoy a homage no vanity could resist.

67

The pioneer women themselves remembered their own rarity very poignantly, often from the standpoint of lack of friends.

> Women were scarce in those days [Mrs. Lucrezia Wilson recalls of the winter 1849–50]. I lived six months in Sacramento and saw only two. There may have been others, but I never saw them. There was no time for visiting or gossiping; it was hard work from daylight till dark, and sometimes long after. . . .

The key phrase here is "no time." There were others, all right, but this drudging boardinghouse keeper of course did not see them. Franklin Buck writes home about a grand ball in Sacramento in April, 1850:

> One of the committee told me that they had issued invitations to *one hundred ladies*. So you see the *sex* are not so few and far between here as you might suppose. [Italics are Buck's] I have no doubt by fall they will glut the market, as is the case with lumber.

Alonzo Delano makes almost the identical comment a year later:

> They are of but little account here, and although there is quite a rush of them from the States, they . . . will be compelled to work for a living at from fifty to a hundred dollars per month on their arrival. They had better stay at home.

By that time being female wasn't sufficient—a woman would have to work like any other settler.

Nevertheless, Mrs. Wilson told what was true in her own experience when she said there were almost no women in town. Even if she had had time to wander about the city, her path would not have intersected theirs, and she had no time. The demands of men and work kept her eyes fixed on the tiny circle of her own squirrel cage. Every decent woman in early California found herself working like a slave to supply male physical needs unrelated to sex and social life: cooking, baking, washing, scrubbing. The need for cooks and laundresses—for all the services housewives usually provided—was so vast, and the supply so meager, and the monetary rewards so tempting. A year or so later—when frontier conditions in some mining towns still paralleled those of Sacramento in '49—Mrs. Phelps, the first woman in Nevada City, struck gold her own way by selling dried-apple pies at a dollar each. No matter how hard she labored, she could not keep supply up to the level of demand, and miners played euchre Sundays outside her door to determine who should pay for the pies. When the number of women reached the total of five, "had they put themselves up on exhibition, they would have drawn great houses." (Many untalented actresses *did* draw great houses on this account alone.)

To this, Mrs. Wilson, the Sacramento boardinghouse keeper, added:

> Every man thought every woman in that day a beauty.
> Even I have had men come forty miles over the mountains,
> just to look at me, and I never was called a handsome woman,
> in my best days, even by my most ardent admirers.

The author of this wistful comment, like the rest of the wives and mothers, didn't have five spare minutes a day to make herself handsome, even if she had had the materials and the wish to do so. These women—moved not only by the desire to earn money legitimately, but also by a great pity for the homesick men around them and a natural vanity-response to the exaggerated admiration given them—worked

69

hard and purposefully to create homes and "improve society." They used themselves up this way and had nothing left over for frills.

Though the chronicler of Sonora, William Perkins, noted large numbers of women in the country as early as 1849, he wrote of a visit to Stockton in 1851: "For the first time in California, I have enjoyed the society of respectable women and romped with white curly headed Saxon children."

This unique event he recorded in two sentences. Writing two years earlier, he devoted half a page to a description of the way the señoritas dressed:

> The Mexican beauty wears a rich skirt trimmed with laborious worked flounces, satin shoes, flesh colored silk stockings and a gloriously bespangled shawl, glistering with all the chinese arts of embroidery and colors. In the street, the shawl is drawn over the head and thrown over the left shoulder very gracefully. In the house it is worn more negligently and the bosom is very freely exposed as they wear no body to their dresses.

We cannot be sure whether the señoritas actually wore nothing above the waist except the highly versatile shawl (or silk *rebozo*, for Sundays), or whether as seems likely they wore some sort of camisole top, ignored by the interested male as merely a kind of underwear. The point is that again and again, this Canadian sojourner devoted pages to Mexican and French women, giving their habits, dress and morals a careful and detailed analysis in a manner fascinated even when it seemed most critical.

But to this notable occasion—his first meeting with a respectable woman—he devoted exactly five lines of his journal.

The woman in the sunbonnet was one of the most respected figures of her day. Forty-niners, almost as if overreacting to the value

70

of her virtue while enjoying the lack of virtue in others, treated her with abject chivalry; never was a woman so worshiped, so jealously guarded. The record of the period and the judgment of history grant her the medal of honor over and over again.

Nevertheless, the grinding labor of making a home in the wilderness did nothing to improve her personal attractiveness. What little time she had for sponsoring social life she very often used to declare half the women in town "off limits" for the respectable dancing party she was patronizing. This was something like taking candy from babies. Just the same, the forty-niner was absolutely required to believe in her and value her far above the "wrong kind of woman" who didn't make her invitation list.

But while the sunbonnets went on slowly carving the frontier into civilized shape, the ranking courtesans of San Francisco continued to be the equal, in charm and beauty, of courtesans anywhere in the world. The women who wore the harlequin masques at the notorious masquerade balls of the fifties were lovely and perfumed, gaudy and painted and not in the least cold-hearted or unsympathetic toward man's base nature. They represented luxury, they represented fun, and they did not represent responsibility. They belonged to a class not quite human—the class of commodities rather than persons—but so, in another way, did all women, and at least they made a rather good thing of it. They had leisure, unlike the sunbonnets, for learning the art of pleasing men as women, not as cooks. They had to learn it well, for their living depended on it, as the wife's did not. Certainly they were fallen—but they were lively, they were entertaining, and they were *there*.

The Frenchwoman who presided at lansquenet was a cold-hearted devil—a man killed in front of her meant very little to her—but, unless she already belonged to the gambler who ran the place, she was there for you. The dark girl with the *rebozo* over her black hair, not shrewd like mademoiselle, not schooled for charming like the masquer, was by her own nature passive, willing, tropically warm—and, providing you could avoid her Mexican protectors, she was there for you.

But the sunbonnet mother wasn't there for you, except as a figure of worship; and where fun was to be had, she had little time to be present—her hearth and her nursery were sufficient to use her up.

Many an Argonaut, having his first taste of a life planets apart from the narrow walled-in elm-lined world of a Vermont town where the shadow of the church steeple stretched to the city limits, was torn between what he knew he had to like and what he could not admit he really liked.

Thus in the opening years of the golden era, the sunbonnets marched slowly into first the cities and then the remote villages; and at the same time, with a great thrust of conquest, the easy women poured off the ships and settled where the prospects looked richest, in urban centers and in towns like Sonora where Yankee Puritanism was weakest. The battle lines were drawn between the sunbonnet women in their kitchens and the women of masque and *rebozo* in their fandango houses and gambling hells. Each, moving unself-consciously in her own prescribed circle, had little awareness of this conflict, of the way in which these circles that never could intersect nevertheless rubbed against each other. In the friction so generated—hardly recognized but everywhere present—many a hitherto unthinking American man had to re-examine his attitudes towards women in general and sometimes to change those attitudes more than he realized or wished.

"Virtue plodded through the streets bearing burdens," wrote Frank Soulé, "while prostitutes, lauded and caressed, became the leading conservators of social life, fanning its ephemeral brightness by a magnificent display of their presence and deceitful smiles."

One cannot help asking the question—there is too little evidence for a conclusive answer, as America was not yet survey-minded—but one may ask: Wasn't there here, in California of the fifties, a small premature upflaring of a change in moral climate that burst to bonfire proportions nationally in the Freudian, flaming-youth twenties? Could a black-and-white, good-or-bad, categorical Puritanism once so shaken and challenged by masque and *rebozo* ever return entirely to its previous state of God-given certainty about what Woman was and had to be?

CHAPTER 7

"The House of the Strange Woman"

A little further on was "the house of the strange woman," magnificent without, beautiful within, furnished with Brussels, velvet, silk, and damask. Heavy furniture of rosewood, and walls hung with beautiful paintings; and music from the pianoforte, melodeon, and harp; no house more prominent or beautiful for situation in the city.

—Rev. William Taylor.

ALTHOUGH STREET-PREACHER TAYLOR REPEATEDLY CALLED THE IM-PENITENT MAGDALENE BY THE ADJECTIVE "STRANGE"—AND ALTHOUGH she was generally designated this way, in an attempt to avoid offending Victorian taste with the simple word prostitute—she was nothing like as strange to him and other moralists of the time as she is to those of the twentieth century who would assess her character and position in gold rush society. The categorical imperative of Victorian morals made her a stock figure of comparative simplicity: lost, abandoned, an impersonation of the devil who fought earnest shepherds like the Reverend Mr. Taylor for the souls of men.

But she was not a single, simple type. Like the gambler who was her companion in the business of preying upon the Argonaut, she was a uniform type only in the primary fact that she played on the wrong side of the fence. Within this classification one finds women ranging from the cultivated, sophisticated Parisienne to the most miserable slave of the Chinese alleys, a creature scarcely a step removed from animal level. These were not a standard item labeled "fallen women." These were human beings in all the variety that human beings are capable of assuming, in spite of the fact that around them ran a fine invisible line corralling them away from decent women and all the considerations required by decent women.

Before discussing the tremendous differences that existed among these women, it would be good to know how many sinners there actually were in proportion to respectable maids and matrons. Here the shakiness of population statistics and the complete lack of population analysis prevents anything but a guess. That guess, however, can be based on what contemporaries had to say.

Before the gold rush, the estimated population of California was only around fourteen thousand, over half of whom were Spanish-descended. Most of the Americans belonged to the occupying forces left over from the Mexican War. True professional prostitutes were probably scarce, though native girls, from a soldier's viewpoint, did not come under the restrictions that custom imposed on relations with civilized women. The Mexican girls must have been difficult to liberate, however, for the native dons were notoriously jealous.

The estimated population in the middle of 1850 was well over a hundred thousand, almost two-thirds American. Of this number at least seven eighths were men. The total number of women and children, concentrated mostly in cities, could not have been much over thirteen thousand. Since most pioneer wives had children with them, it is safe to guess there must have been three to five thousand children making part of this total. We can assume that by the end of 1850 there could not have been many over ten thousand women in California, and the figure may have been lower.

The tide of female fortune hunters began in 1849, increased in 1850 and 1851, and after that—due in part to the later-starting mass immigration of wives and families—ceased to be proportionally large. Most miners gave themselves about two years to "make their pile" and go home. If they decided not to go home, they sent for their families. This settling process was well under way by 1851 and had grown to important proportions by 1854. By that year San Francisco alone had a registration of school children numbering better than twenty-five hundred, which was seventy percent of all children in the city over four years old. This indicates that unquestionably by then the influx of wives brought their ranks to a number many times that of the street women, at least in the urban areas. Numerically they had the situation well in hand by the mid-fifties.

But they could not have had this quantitative edge on the mavericks in the years 1849–51. During 1850 Frank Soulé claimed two thousand women entered the state, "many of whom were of base character and loose practices." Two notable native Californians, José Fernandez who was first Alcalde of San Jose under American rule, and General Mariano Vallejo, both observant educated men who watched the change-over period with analytical eyes, commented on the feminine invasion in a way that supports Soulé's cynicism.

According to Fernandez, the first two years brought from Mexico, France and Peru an "infinity of prostitutes." The Mexican women did not pay passage, but were sold by the ship captains to the highest bidder when they reached San Francisco. Then they worked out their price in the fandango houses which, as all students of white-slave practices are aware, took a long, long time.

French courtesans got their ship passage free also, but the ar-rangement was different. The French government, anxious to unload its excess stock, conducted a great lottery for bars of gold. The profits of the lottery were used to pay passage for three hundred prostitutes and their masculine business associates. This does not mean there were only three hundred—the number includes the women involved in this particular deal, not the free-lance ones.

According to Fernandez:

> The French women did much more damage to the public morals than did the Mexicans, because these ex-Parisian sirens, more skilled in the art of entrapping the unwary, in place of allowing themselves to be kept in large houses, where they must share their earnings with the proprietors, rented the best apartments. From these they sallied forth at noon to preside over some table of monte or lansquinet. It is not too much to say that half of the money of which the gamblers robbed the miners and merchants went into the pockets of the sylph-like seductresses who presided over the game.

This is only a guess, but it is a safe one considering the shrewdness of the mademoiselles and the shortage of women. They worked of course in partnership with the French gamblers who acted as their pimps and protectors, but they were almost never forced into the white-slavery conditions that existed among many prostitutes of other nationalities. They were the aristocracy of the profession.

South American prostitutes came in from Chile, last port before the Isthmus, and were classed by the Yankees along with all women from that country as "Chileños." Like other Latin-American women of this caste, they were mostly excellent dancers and general entertainers, but they seldom had the comparative business freedom of mademoiselle. They were usually in houses; sometimes if they were pretty enough they functioned as mistresses.

General Vallejo claimed France sent over "several thousand lying men and corrupt women" at the expense of the government, which sounds like an exasperated exaggeration. He also commented on the immigration of Chinese—among whom prostitutes were unconditional slaves—and blamed them for harm to the health and morals of San Francisco, claiming they "had made it a duty to keep the hospitals always filled with syphilitics."

William Perkins made constant reference to new batches of women arriving in Sonora, starting early in 1849 with the entrance of numerous Peruvians and Chileños who naturally sought the one town in the gold country where Latin people predominated. In the spring of 1850 he discovered women "are pouring in like a general immigration." A typical entry in his journal, near the end of that year, stated:

> Sonora has just been honored and beautified by the arrival of a bevy of fair and frail damsels who have come up with the laudible design of easing the miners of their hard-earned gold-dust. They are a bad set and last night a serious row took place in the house where they are lodged, and some men were badly hurt.

Perkins, being Canadian, did not suffer from the excesses of a New England conscience and got along very well with most of the ladies; so if he says this crowd was "a bad set," they must have been troublesome indeed. Most of the free-lance girls, as contrasted with the protected mistress group, did cause a great deal of brawling for obvious reasons.

William Perkins analyzed his new friends carefully from the standpoint of nationality. He summed up several pages on the subject with the statement:

> The Spaniard in all circumstances remains a "Woman" with all the feminine qualities pertaining to her sex: warm hearted, generous and unartificial. The Frenchwoman is made up of artificiality; profligate, shameless, avaricious and vain, she studiously covers these defects with a charming

manner, fascinating conversation and a deportment before the world which is unexceptionable. She is the Apple of the shore of the Dead Sea—enchanting on the exterior, within a mass of filth.

Finally he got around to Anglo-Saxon prostitutes, categorizing them in a sentence: "Of the English women from Sydney and the loose American women from the States, I say nothing; vulgar, degraded and brutish as they are in their own countries, a trip to California has not, of course, improved them."

Apparently the Yankee women were not cut out for that life. While nobody else went into as much detail as Perkins, the men in general implied that they rated the French at the top, then the Latins, then Americans and English, and Chinese at the bottom.

All of these comments together do not add up to anything that would impress the people who do statistical surveys. But if the figure "three hundred" is given for one batch of mademoiselles in one year, and the immigration from South American and other sources added to it, a conservative guess would put the total number of available women at somewhere around two thousand. At least one woman in five, in 1850, must have been viable merchandise. But while the over-all proportion of women and children to men is usually stated at one to seven, the proportion of salable females to wifeless forty-niners could not have been much more than one to twenty-five. This situation still made of woman a premium item: to be granted extreme chivalry if she were another Argonaut's wife, and to be battled over if she were frankly on the market.

The misleading thing about this calculation is that prostitutes were not distributed on any such even ratio over the state. They were concentrated in cities, large towns, and areas like Sonora where conditions suited them. Prostitution in the Yankee-dominated mining camps did not follow the big city pattern, and the women who set up house in the mountain towns did not necessarily receive the cordial welcome you would expect. Wrote a pioneer: "For the first twelve months, I think that style of women were wholly supported by married men, and the young men were the only moral ones in the community." (Most of the men, married or not, were in their twenties.) Sometimes the women were driven out of town. Sometimes—as in the case of Rich Bar's Empire Hotel, originally designed as a brothel—their business failed. But even though there were fewer prostitutes in the mountains than there were in the cities, the gold towns held more of them in proportion to married women, because only the boldest and strongest of pioneer wives were equal to the rugged life in the camps.

The high-class sporting woman of San Francisco was as characteristic of her period as baroque furniture and crimson plush. She pre-empted the most luxurious quarters the city could supply and furnished them to suit her personality. Her boudoir was tinted pink or blue, and the subdued brilliance of gilt-framed mirrors, glass chandeliers and dark statuettes lent a somber glitter to the twilight of her rooms. Thick carpets dulled the sound of footsteps. From windows curtained in white lace and heavily draped in red damask, she looked out upon the streets of the city and waited. The chair in which she sat, and the sofa across the room, were deep and soft, richly upholstered. It was a day when the appeal both of women and their setting was based on opulence: the key words were lush, sumptuous, elegant, and the atmosphere was that of a bordello painted by Rubens.

To modern taste it all sounds like too much plum pudding smothered in whipped cream, but it was exactly right for a bearded male, fresh from a crude log hut in an all-masculine wilderness and loaded with nuggets.

In addition to a plush-lined love nest and plenty of leisure, the top-ranking courtesan had a monopoly on other advantages denied to the pioneer housewife. She could paint her face, which a decent woman could not, and she could make lavish use of perfume—not lavendar sachet, but heavy musky scents supposed to be irresistible. She could afford to ride fast horses through the thoroughfares— often astride, when proper women rode sidesaddle, which was a great help with California horses unaccustomed to sedate bridle paths— and she had spare time to promenade the streets in flaunting luxury while honest women were too overworked to step outside their doors. Though it was impossible for a good woman to be seen in the drinking houses frequented by her husband, the courtesan was always welcome there. No wonder a common gold rush proverb maintained that the only aristocracy in California was made up of gamblers and prostitutes! For these could afford to be aristocratic: they, more than any other class, reaped the golden harvest after the forty-niner had run the harvester through the gold fields.

Since the sunbonnet women were busy and housebound, the role of promoting parties and social life fell by default to Madame and her ladies. When Madame gave a "soiree," she sent out invitations on embossed French stationery to all the important gentlemen—mayor, aldermen, collector of the port, judges, and most particularly members of San Jose's "legislature of a thousand drinks." She engaged the finest caterers and the sprightliest of dance bands. Over the thick carpet whirled politician and underworld queen, dignified judge and painted lady. The girls were on their best behavior—nothing unseemly, all proprieties observed. In fact, as Frank Soulé commented, "were it not for the greater proportion of beauty present" you would think you danced among the blue bloods of the town.

After the dance came supper: oysters, strawberries, all the delicacies of the season. Nobody paid for anything but the champagne—

81

and that was ten dollars a bottle. As she could probably sell twelve dozen bottles to a thirsty crowd urged on by beautiful girls, Madame hardly stood to lose.

But even if she had lost financially, she could chalk it up to advertising—and protection. Small chance the judge who danced at her soiree would sentence her girls to the house of correction.

In the towns, as in the cities, the reigning courtesans commanded the best of everything that money could buy and were usually among the first to own expensive scarcity items. Yankee trader Frank Buck wrote home from Weaverville that he had received the music his family sent him, but there was only one piano in town upon which to play it and that was in a brothel. "We are not able to have them plentifully as yet," he explained, and added "(I mean the pianos.)" Whether or not he was ever able to play the music, he did not say.

But if the wealthy courtesan was an aristocrat, her unlucky sister in sin was as different from her as a toiling camptown drudge from a Park Avenue hostess. The man who struck it rich sought out the plushy dens of mademoiselle; the poor man, or the man who'd already lost his dust at the green table, was no friend of hers.

The poor man's brothel was known as a fandango house, or sometimes a dance cellar because it was so often located in a basement. It was a Mexican institution to start with (all Latin-inspired dances were lumped together by Yankees as "fandango") but its make-up was not necessarily Mexican. A few of the dance cellars were Negro houses, and many were predominantly stocked with the indentured women off the ships from Peru and Chile. They were supposed to have a non-Anglo-Saxon flavor, whatever the mixture of races and nationalities might be.

According to widely quoted statistics gathered by the *Christian Advocate,* San Francisco supported forty-eight houses "kept by bawds" in 1853. Most of them were located on Jackson, Pacific and Commercial streets, among the gambling hells and pawnshops. Pawnshops were strategically sprinkled all through this area because their owners could count on plenty of customers who needed money badly right now.

Some of the fandango houses gave the good citizens quite a bit of trouble. When the music kept up until four in the morning at the Neptune House, neighbors—like neighbors anywhere, any time—called the police. The police hauled Madame into court and said some very harsh words to her. When a Spanish house in the same neighborhood was raided, thirty revelers rode off to the station house. As time went on the police records show an increase in this kind of activity out of proportion to the probable increase of fandango houses, but definitely related to the increase of God-fearing, sleep-craving neighbors with votes.

Most wretched, farthest removed from the Cyprians of the brownstone fronts were the Chinese slaves. The so-called "Celestial" females were bought and sold on the waterfront with less consideration than a careful stockman would give to a deal in cattle. So grotesque and pitiable were these creatures, so wretched the tiny cribs in which they plied their trade, that they severely shocked the good people of California. Many attempts were made to get rid of them, for their presence was an eyesore and an embarrassment to the judges and legislators who kept Mademoiselle in luxury in her excellent neighborhood.

These were not the kind of frail ladies who found their way into the legend of the gold rush adventuress. Much more to the raconteur's liking was the tale of a camptown sporting woman named Swan.

In a certain mining camp, two brothers fell victim to the mountain fever. A passing prospector brought the sad news of their disaster into a gambling hell where beautiful dark-haired Swan was dealing monte. One was already dead, he reported, and the other soon would be. Swan's hands moved more slowly as he spoke, and when he finished she threw down her cards, seized a hat from a miner's head and jumped up on the green table.

Throwing into the hat a handful of nuggets from her own purse, "Swan is sorry so much," she cried—naming a sum liberal even for those days—"Boys, how much are you sorry?" Everyone was "sorry" by substantial amounts. When all had contributed, she went out of the saloon lugging the heavy hat with one hand and holding her wide skirt out of the mire with the other. Making the rounds of the saloons, she quickly collected a small fortune.

Then she took a doctor with her to the tent of the young adventurers. She laid out the dead boy for burial and turned all her energies to nursing his brother back to health.

When at last the miner recuperated, Swan lectured him like a maiden aunt for risking his life in this land of sin and fever, presented him with a ticket to New York and sent him home to mother with a purse full of the gold remaining from the collection.

Swan didn't know Bret Harte and his brethren were watching her every move, but she couldn't have done better if she had known it.

It was as Swan that the prospector liked to think of the woman he visited on Saturday night and forgot on Sunday morning when he wrote his laborious letter home. He much preferred her to her sister who asked a man to treat at the bar, took his money and drew a knife from her stocking if he protested; or the girl who rolled a man for his nuggets and left him with nothing to remember her by but a hangover and wounded vanity. He did not like to think of Mlle. Virginie, who could tell the story of a man killed in front of her with all kinds of eye-rolling emphasis, but never stop dealing lansquenet as she told it.

He could not afford to be permanently disgusted with Mlle. Virginie, but he could forget her in favor of Swan.

And it was Swan—not the Chinese slave, not the icehearted mademoiselle, not the thieving ugly whore at the fandango house—that the forty-niner wove into his mythology. She was the girl he remembered when men sat around their campfires, when the bottle was going around and the folklore of the golden era was cooking. Certainly many of the fallen ones, like many of the respectable ones, had warm hearts and quick sympathy for the unfortunate. From these, the writers who later sprayed gilt over the rough rocky ore of the early fifties created their famous stereotype of prostitute-with-heart-of-gold.

But when you finish looking over the field of women for sale—when you have taken note of lush courtesan, fandango girl, gun-toting vixen, bedraggled slave—you have not exhausted the categories of maverick females. There was another large class of women who were not respectable, but were not strictly prostitutes either, though of course they classed with "fallen women" because they were not legal wives. Belle Cora, mistress of the gambler Charles Cora, was of this level. She became a newspaper sensation after Cora was arrested by the Vigilance Committee of '56 for shooting a man who had insulted Belle. She mustered all the money and influence she could and fought his conviction for a long time. When his death by hanging became inevitable, she was legally married to him just before the hangmen carried out the sentence. No lawful wife could have been more faithful or doggedly determined to save her man—yet Belle Cora was a notorious creature whose appearance in a theater audience where decent women were seated was the breach of convention that touched off the shooting.

Some of the women in the mistress class had been kept by one man or another for more years than they could remember. Others strayed into this caste from the order of "respectable women" when the freedom of California and the gold offerings of eager Argonauts lured them into jumping the fence. Most of the records are reticent on this subject and supply no details, except cries of alarm about the poisonous influence of California's moral climate. But divorce statistics and anecdotes of runaway wives and seduced daughters give the definite impression that a minor but fairly steady erosion nibbled at the edges of respectable womanhood.

When Perkins spoke of Sonora's "inundation" of women in the spring of 1850, he added that women were so plentiful "Every man may have a wife if he chooses. As yet however, we have no 'wives' in California. Thousands of women there are but they are all mistresses or independent. This state is so common that it excites no remark. The mistress occupies here the same position that the wife does in other countries and most of the women are of a class that think it no disgrace." (He spoke from his limited perspective, of course; there *were* wives in California, but not many.)

Perkins explained that the señoritas and the mademoiselles both preferred this arrangement to the one blessed by the priest: the Mexican would not marry a "heretic" but would live with him; the Frenchwoman refused to bind herself by ties she knew her natural temperament would soon incline her to break. Both were faithful and happy companions, the informant claimed, as long as they were well treated or until they got interested in another man.

Later, speaking of new arrivals, he admitted there were "some honest women amongst them, but . . . they are few, and certainly the least prepossessing." Most of the semipermanent couples paid lip service to the proprieties by passing themselves off as married; and although everyone knew they were not, the little fantasy was accepted as a face-saving device both for the couple and for society in general

—as a married couple, they could be "received in respectable society," but if they were openly sinful the American men of Sonora might feel qualms about associating with them.

From his wide acquaintance with mademoiselles and his fascinated analysis of their character, Perkins concluded that "Within a certain circle in France, the motto of married women appears to be faithlessness to the husband and truth to the lover; and this fact has made more common the eschewing of the marriage ceremony." The free contract had great advantages, since it lasted only as long as both parties were happy with the arrangement. Knowledge of a lover's legal freedom to desert at any time meant that each person was extremely careful to be good to the other. Perkins insisted that he did not, of course, condone such conduct; he merely repeated what the French had told him.

There is no way of knowing how widespread, outside the cosmopolitan air of Sonora, was the custom of maintaining a common-law mate in an arrangement that passed socially as marriage. It was definitely not an American notion of how to treat a woman: you either used her, or you married her, respected her and worked her to death. Still there were cases among Americans in the mines of runaway couples from the East who had joined the gold rush as part of their elopement plan and passed in the new country as man and wife.

Observation of these heathen customs could not help but influence the more impressionable emigrants from the States. "It too often happens here," commented Alonzo Delano in his letters to the home papers, "that females who have borne unexceptionable characters at home adopt the code of morals of the country and instead of endeavoring to stem the current, float along with it."

How many women floated along with that current and how many fought to stem it will be something to examine later, when the shift

87

in population types increased the influence of Victorian womanhood. The years 1849–51 were not her years; her ranks were still too meager and spread too thin among the cabins of the Sierra and the frame houses springing up on the sand hills of San Francisco.

The dark girl in the *rebozo*, the shrewd wench with the masque, and mademoiselle at her green table held the center of the golden stage, and sunbonnet girls still waited in the wings.

CHAPTER *8*

Jeems Pipes and Yankee Robinson

WHEN THE CURTAIN WENT UP ON THE FIRST "CONCERT" IN CALIFOR-
NIA, OFFICIALLY OPENING WHAT WOULD BECOME A RICH AND MADCAP
theater, no woman waited in the wings. Actually there were no wings,
for the theater was San Francisco's one-room schoolhouse on the
Plaza, which also doubled as a jail. And the lone entertainer was
Steve Massett, self-styled "Jeems Pipes of Pipesville," mimic and
song writer, monologuist and newspaper columnist, and general roust-
about of the promotion world.

Newspaper advertisements trumpeted the concert in gaudy prose:
Jeems would produce his inimitable one-man show on June 22, 1849.
When the evening arrived, the schoolhouse was so crowded the men
almost had to breathe in unison.

But there was room and to spare for the women—all four of
them. The whole front row was optimistically "reserved for ladies,"
and not the least exciting part of the show was the moment before the
curtain rose when the women paraded majestically to the front of the
house and settled their voluminous skirts upon their special bench.

Steve Massett stepped forward and glanced out over the smoky
little room crammed with beards and red flannel shirts; and the
whiskery ones craned their necks and twisted to get a good look at
their entertainer. They saw a round little Englishman, with a red

89

face crowned by coppery curls, beaming and jovial and just a trace overwhelmed by his own audacity. He sat down at the only piano in California and led off with his song (words and music by Steve Massett), "When the Moon on the Lake is Beaming." The rest of the evening he alternated sentimental ballads of his own composition, a falsetto burlesque of opera star Anna Bishop, and skits in which he played all the parts. He was at his best as an imitator, and the audience was almost pitifully appreciative when he gave them his version of the standard stage types of the era. They clapped wildly for his recitation of "The Frenchman, the Exquisite and the Yankee in Richard III," and roared their approval for his imitation of a German girl and an elderly spinster trying out for a spot in a Massachusetts choir.

The success of this venture was due less to Steve's actual talents than to the fact that his was the only show in town. It was not immediately repeated. Show business collapsed into its previous state of desuetude, and was not heard from again until it suddenly came to life that October in Sacramento.

In a board-and-canvas hall flung up in back of the Round Tent gambling saloon, the Eagle Stock Company—first of its kind in the state—opened with *The Bandit Chief; or, the Forest Spectre,* and continued with horrific renditions of *The Wife, The Rivals,* and *Charles the Second.* Customers entered through the Round Tent, getting well fortified on the way, sometimes losing their ticket money to the monte dealer before they got as far as the box office. Three dollars admitted them to the "boxes," a rough gallery at one end of the room, precariously bearing nearly a hundred people; for only two dollars, they could scramble for sitting space on the benches of the bare hollow which was the pit. Between acts they cleared a little space on these benches and played a quick round of monte while they waited for the show to go on.

90

From the moment the brown, yellow and lilac curtain rose, the Eagles were a howling success. Night after night the miners came to loll on the splintery benches, exploding with mirth over blood-and-thunder melodrama, greeting tender love scenes with whistles and catcalls. The mood of the forty-niners called for broad comedy above all—and subsequent theatrical ventures showed that the prize nuggets went to the performers who guessed right about their basic preference for slapstick rather than sentiment, drama, or Art. (This didn't stop them from worshiping all actresses and crowding to see any play, even Shakespeare.) If the stock company did not give them comedy, they chose to take the melodrama as if it were a burlesque of itself, which the acting talents of the performers undoubtedly warranted. The actors were coining money anyway, and if the miners were determined to take their attempts at tragedies in that spirit, still they were troupers and they carried on gallantly above the raucous groans and whistles.

Gallant as they were, they were no match for the California climate. It rained all fall, it rained all December, and in January of 1850, it really rained.

If you had entered the Eagle Theater one soggy evening that month, you would have been glad to escape from the streaming streets to the comparative shelter of the playhouse. But your pleasure would have been short-lived. The water crept snakelike up from the Sacramento River. Before the first part of the program was done, water glistened through the cracks in the board floor. By the time the second act was well under way, every man in the pit was standing on a bench to keep his feet dry. Later the whooping pioneers scrambled up away from the rapidly rising tide and perched upon the railings of the gallery, dangling booted feet over the turgid stream as the play came to a surging climax.

The Eagles held out as stubbornly against high water as they previously had against hell. For several nights the show went on for an audience that hung from the rafters over that portion of the Sacramento River now serving as the Eagle Theater. On January fourth the company owned itself washed out and floated down the river to San Francisco.

A few weeks later promoters prudently built the next Sacramento Theater, the Tehama, on high ground. This one opened with a stock company headed by an actress named Mrs. Kirby, whose claim to fame was rather peculiar. Her first husband, whose name she retained at this time for professional purposes, was an English actor so noted for his dramatic death throes that the phrase initiated by bored gallery gods, "Wake me up when Kirby dies," became a catchword. Kirby needed the practice, as it turned out: he was only twenty-nine when he put in his final performance, offstage and for keeps. The phrase pursued his widow, as an identifying tag, and, by one of those ironical grace notes of history, proved all too appropriate.

When she arrived in San Francisco in January, 1850, she brought husband number two, a Mr. Wingate. Fortunately she did not take his name, for in the autumn of that same year Mr. Wingate left her by way of a fatal ride on a murderous horse. This put Mrs. Kirby off the stage for a week and out of the marriage business for six months. Then she married James Stark, a leading actor and manager in San Francisco. He survived to be divorced some years later, placing third in a husband series of five. She outlived the other two. Stark was the only one who lived to be left. Mrs. Kirby made it up to him by adopting his name as her stage name, and so became famous as Mrs. Stark. It is so that she appears in California stage history.

Husbands were not the only people who found Mrs. Stark fatally overpowering. When Mrs. John Hambleton, of the Stark company, poisoned herself early in 1851, the incident appeared at first as a routine triangle. Mrs. Hambleton loved another member of the company, Mr. Coad, and after her wronged husband confronted the guilty pair, there was nothing for the sinning heroine to do but swallow the lethal dose. All this was completely nineteenth century and closely patterned after the stock melodramas in which these people performed night after night—so closely that it almost looked like nature aping Art.

But here the plot got slightly off the track. Mr. Hambleton sent outraged letters to the newspapers, accusing Mrs. Stark of his wife's death. It was all her fault, because Mrs. Stark had advised Mrs. Hambleton, woman to woman, that married to a brute like John her only recourse was to take the eager Mr. Coad for her lover. Therefore, Mrs. Stark had instilled the venom that led to the poor innocent wife's untimely death. Mrs. Stark admitted in the newspapers that John was indeed a brute, but claimed that she herself had no guilt in the matter because she had merely, as sympathetic confidant of the late Mrs. Hambleton, stated this obvious truth. If it had not been a phrase too awkward for a slogan, the gallery gods who watched the real-life affairs of actors unfold might well have put it, 'Wake me up when practically anyone involved with Mrs. Kirby-Stark dies."

Mrs. Stark began her notorious San Francisco career in Rowe's Amphitheatre, a huge tent on Kearny Street (capacity fifteen hundred) which Colonel Rowe erected for his circus. Rowe opened his show in October, 1849, and vied with Steve Massett and the Eagle Stock Company for the honor of providing the state's first entertainment. Circus was the rage of San Francisco late in 1849, especially as Mrs. Rowe was an accomplished and shapely equestrienne. The city even had two circuses when Rowe's clown, Foley, gave notice (he couldn't live on twelve hundred a month salary) and opened his own company. But the forty-niner's mercurial favor already veered toward drama, so the Colonel thought of a compromise. He got in touch with some of the actors who had been flooded out by the Sacramento River and introduced the new improved circus (with classical drama added) in February, 1850, with *Othello*.

Unfortunately, the circus could not stay off the stage: Shakespeare's gloomy Moor brooded and agonized in the center ring while all around him clowns leaped over horses and strong men exhibited their muscles. The marriage of drama and circus proved a hopeless *mésalliance*. The circus decided to tour the diggings, and legitimate actors rushed around hunting jobs, doing one-night stands, and contributing to an atmosphere of wild promotion schemes.

That spring of 1850 all kinds of little theatrical projects sizzled and popped all over the state like bubbles in the mud pots at Yellowstone Park. It was the season of the big warm-up for the chaotic, effervescent, breathless scramble that the San Francisco theater of the fifties was about to become.

One of the stars warming up that season was Yankee Robinson, legitimately bearing the title of Doctor because he was a graduate physician and had been making a living in his drugstore on the Plaza since 1847. At this time San Francisco had a big eager audience and no theater to speak of; Dr. Robinson had a keen wit, vast if loose-hung powers of creative imagination and an impassioned zeal for promoting. Accordingly he located a little room on a side street and manufactured a theater from nothing. Having no paints, he plastered his backdrop with mustard and curry. Against this sickly background he competed with Steve Massett in song-and-dance routines, Yankee impersonations and the other one-man tricks of the time.

An important factor in the rapid and almost magical improvement of San Francisco theaters was the circumstance that great fires periodically razed the city. There was no excuse for hanging on to a decrepit tent and promising yourself one of these days you'd have a real playhouse. Not only was there no excuse to do this, there was no chance to do it. Every few months, or even weeks, fire leveled the town and forced all impresarios to start over again from nothing, or get out of the business. And the business was worth staying in because the amusement-mad Argonauts, escapists in the first place, would pay high for any entertainment that provided escape from the new pressures California had put upon them. Whether at this time show business was a civilizing influence on them or they were a disruptive influence in theater would be hard to say. It worked both ways.

The brash angular little doctor was not one to be driven out of business when the May 1850 fire ate up his mustard-plastered hall. On the Fourth of July he and his partner opened the Robinson and Evrard Museum, skyrocketing to glory with the first smash hit of the California stage, *Seeing the Elephant.*

Doctor Robinson, it seems, had more than a quick wit and a ready tongue: he had an angle. He must have picked up his special angle from the air, sniffing it out the way a bloodhound can pick up a special track from a tangle of useless ones. What he discovered was that the subject the miners most readily laughed at was the ridiculous spectacle of the forty-niner advancing to conquer El Dorado and getting thrown back on the seat of his pants. Many a comic since has cashed in on the curious fact that the human animal gets a perverse satisfaction out of laughing at himself. Doctor Robinson made the idea pay off in a big way with his opening skit, and he never stopped working the same vein until the claim played out on him.

The Doctor didn't write this play himself, to begin with, though

95

by the time he finished rewriting it and ad-libbing it into new shape at his Museum, it was hard to tell where Robinson left off and the Elephant began. The skit was given first in New York City, by Easterners ridiculing the gold rush; once before it had been tried in California, but without any attempt to alter it to suit the California scene which it claimed as its locale.

Robinson took the skeletal plot—which was nothing, after all, but the sad tale everybody knew about the man who fell in love with Trouble and won her—and stuffed it full of clever topical references like a housewife camouflaging an economy cake batter with a fistful of raisins. It was broad burlesque, aimed straight at the roughhewn creature in the flannel shirt who handed over his dust for a front-row seat; it hit him where he lived and he paid for the privilege of being the target.

Noting this, the Doctor quickly dug from his claim another nugget: the topical song. Mostly his songs satirized the miners; sometimes they struck deeply into the foibles of local political figures. The politicians, thinking perhaps to draw his fangs, allowed popular demand to make him San Francisco alderman that year.

The miners apparently rolled in the aisles every time the Doctor poked his sharp finger into their idiosyncracies, their failures, their disappointments. One of the songs they picked up from his repertoire was the wailing tale of woe, "The Used-up Miner," which went in part:

> Oh, I ha'nt got no home, nor nothing else, I s'pose,
> Misfortune seems to follow me wherever I goes,
> I come to California with a heart both stout and bold
> And I've been up to the diggin's there to get some lumps of
>   gold.
> Oh, I'm a used-up man, a perfect used-up man,
> And if I ever get home again,
> I'll stay there if I can.

He'd stay there if he could, but he doubted if he could: for all his wailing self-pity, actually he was having a big time right where he was, and part of that big time he was having in the Doctor's Museum. One thing he liked was the privilege of talking back to the Doctor—it was perfectly all right to shout his criticisms out loud at the moment he thought of them. The Doctor didn't get angry—he was no high priest of the True Drama—he ad-libbed fresh insults right back, and in this way the play at the Museum took on something of the atmosphere of an audience-participation show. The forty-niner felt that this was his own theater and he was part of it. But even as he laughed at the absurd picture he saw in the mirror Yankee Robinson held up, he rubbed an uneasy hand over the whiskered countenance, a little self-conscious, a little uneasy about the loud, crude, uncultured character he had become in this country where no woman could make him shave, wash, go to church, put on a clean shirt or get up in the morning if he didn't want to.

Robinson was exactly the right fellow for a stag audience. The more wives and mothers poured into San Francisco, the lower sank his personal star. There were, of course, many other reasons for his decline, including a fearful clash with Mrs. Stark and the rise of Tom Maguire as boss-man of San Francisco's impresarios. But one can guess he did not have the right kind of appeal for the ladies, anyway.

He certainly did not appeal to Mary Jane Megquier, who lived in the same boardinghouse with Dr. Robinson and his wife. Throughout her letters to her family, Mary Jane makes snide references to him, climaxing her sniping comments with a statement one would not expect a proper Victorian lady to put down on paper. (Mrs. Megquier was rapidly going native and losing her New England accent.)

"I was up at Mrs Robinson last night," she wrote to her daughter;

"the Dr said he was coming down to get some medicine for his wife, she was sick at her stomach in the morning. I told him it was enough to make any woman sick to sleep with him. . . ."

The Used-up Miner didn't care about this side of Yankee Robinson's personality and continued to love him dearly and keep him in the blue chips as long as the miner himself was the predominant figure in California.

CHAPTER 9

Napoleon Tom Maguire

IN HIS ROOMS UPSTAIRS OVER HIS PARKER HOUSE SALOON, THE FUTURE NAPOLEON OF SAN FRANCISCO'S SHOW BUSINESS COUNTED THE PROFITS from his faro tables and speculated on the fascinating question: what else can I do to help a lonesome miner get rid of his gold?

Tom Maguire, the man who later helped put Yankee Robinson out of business, had been a cabdriver and then a gambler. By September 1949 he had risen another step: he was proprietor of one of the best hells when owning a gambling hell was the best business venture in California. But Tom was never satisfied. He knew no bonanza lasted forever, and it was worth a man's while to consider where his next bonanza might be coming from.

Tom thought he detected a rich new claim. Women as lures were a valuable part of his business, but you could make the supply go farther if the women were actresses performing on a stage, delighting many male eyes at once. And if in time there were numerous nonprofessional women to consider, women among the consumers rather than the suppliers of entertainment, theater would draw them where gambling would not.

Therefore the best gamble in California was a theater, and it would be only fitting for the best theater to be built and managed by the leading gambler. The first Jenny Lind Theater—named for one of the few singers who never came to California—was nothing but the hall upstairs over Tom's saloon, with its face lifted to suit the crimson-

99

plush taste of the period. James Stark was Tom's director, and James put his audience and his cast (including the fatal lady he was to marry and her then-current, short-lived spouse Wingate) through a stiff course of Shakespeare that autumn. *Othello, Richard III, Hamlet* and solemn contemporary problem plays from England sought to draw San Franciscans up from Yankee Robinson's low level of farce to an appreciation of the higher things—duels, tears, ranting theatrical tantrums and all the breast-beating melodrama that was Art in 1850.

Except from the Doctor, Tom had very little competition. Theater was booming all over, but it was fly-by-night stuff. And behind the scenes waited that nemesis of the city, Fire. During 1850 and '51, theaters rose and burned and rose again with pistonlike speed as flames swept six times over the city. The big fire of May 4, 1851, took with it both the Jenny Lind and Robinson's Dramatic Museum. Tent and frame blazed like tinder, and heavy iron buildings, guaranteed fireproof, melted in the intense heat, trapping more than one trusting victim who stayed by his safe and his records and could not at the last escape through swollen iron doors. The city, purged again of its tents and shacks, took for its seal the phoenix, and drove its energies once more into lifting itself from the ashes.

Tom Maguire got to work on his second Jenny Lind Theater so rapidly that he was able to finish the building and get the grand opening over with in time to lose the whole thing in the fire of June 22, 1851.

Working more slowly this time—after all, he could not know that the June fire was the sixth and last of that terrible series, and he would rather lose an unfinished building than a completed one—Tom was ready to open the third Jenny Lind on October 4, 1851, one year after his beginning in the hall over the Parker House.

100

While Tom was between theaters, San Francisco would have been without a playhouse if Yankee Robinson had not immediately rented the only hall left in town—the little French Adelphi Theater, which had been struggling with early attempts at opera—and signed up the Starks. He could do this because the Starks, by now man and wife, had also been cut adrift by fire: the Sacramento fire that burned their own theater there took all other theaters at the same time, leaving them professionally homeless.

So Yankee Robinson and the Starks teemed up to cater to theater lovers while Tom Maguire prepared to bid again for the czar-of-show-business role. The Doctor had to cut his cloth considerably to the requirements of his stars. They played the heavy drama, played it to the hilt of their collapsible stage daggers; the Doctor, a clown dreaming in his heart of epics, had not yet let his dream get the better of his common sense. In his Museum, he had produced in quick succession every play he ever wrote or thought he wrote. One of them was the *Reformed Drunkard,* later famous under the title *Ten Nights in a Barroom.* His descendants claim he was the true author of this, the prototype of "Drunkard" melodramas popular still in burlesque form, and that the manuscript was stolen by villains and put out as *Ten Nights* under different authorship. More likely the piece was the product of Robinson's reworking of somebody's script: he could never touch a play without embroidering his own personality into it so firmly that you couldn't tell the original cloth from the fancywork.

However difficult it was to mesh his broadly satiric talents with the lugubrious solemnities of the Starks, Robinson was a businessman —a businessman educated by his financial troubles with the Museum and its hectic, unrehearsed, scatterbrained performances—and he knew he could not depend solely on the one-string violin of his own satires. The Starks were pulling in the customers all over the state, so the Starks were for him. And he knew he wouldn't have the monopoly of the San Francisco entertainment business for long. The men with the trowels were busy as ants over on the Plaza, putting blocks of yellow sandstone from Australia together for Tom Maguire, setting him up the plushiest playhouse the state had yet seen.

There wasn't a thing the Doctor could do about it at the moment except produce Tom Maguire's opening-night play, *All Is Not Gold that Glitters,* before Tom could get to it.

The new Jenny Lind reigned like a fat prima donna over the Plaza, all three fluted-stone stories. The vast hall—pit, parquet, and four tiers of boxes and gallery seats—would hold three thousand, and did. The walls and ceiling glowed pale pink and burst at intervals into decorous ecstasies of gilt carving. Dress circle and parquet (three dollars a ticket) overflowed with "beauty and fashion" on opening night. Upper boxes, at two dollars, were nearly as showy a location. For one silver dollar you could sit in the pit or the gallery. The pit was for newsboys, sports, and crude customers in general; at the farthest extreme, horizontally speaking, the gallery was "fitted up in elegant style for respectable colored people."

While the custom of segregating customers with dark faces into the topmost rows had not in California reached the level of absolute law, "nigger heavens" were beginning to appear in theaters big enough to afford the luxury. Being stuck in the gallery, the Negroes naturally wanted it to themselves, and thus sometimes segregation proved two-edged. Once when two white men entered the restricted rows, each with a pretty mulatto girl on his arm, the colored people already entrenched there began to mutter and threaten and growl around until the management, fearing a brawl, had to request the pale intruders to go back where they came from.

With the opening of his elegant Jenny Lind, Tom was definitely out in front of the Doctor. He could not stay there long. The men with the trowels were toiling for Robinson now, down along the water front, on Sansome Street. Sansome had recently been not a street but a wharf; by this time the tons of dirt dug from the sand-hills as they were graded for the city had been dumped into the Bay, filling in the shallows along the wharfs. Onto the land thus created the city pushed timidly forward, like an old lady testing the ice in a pond to see if it will hold her.

The cohorts of Tom of course set rumors spinning that Robinson's American Theater, built on the filled-in area, was dangerously unsafe. The Doctor ignored the rumors and got set for a grand first night of his own.

The "I can do anything better than you can" spirit of their rivalry extended to the furnishings of the American. Conceding something because of an exterior built only of brick and wood, and a capacity of only two thousand, the American wouldn't yield an inch in the matter of interior decoration. From a high gilded dome, intricately carved, hung a centerpiece that threw glittering sparks of light from hundreds of glass prisms. Two additional chandeliers, lighting the stage and the front of the pit, swung from the beaks of two rococo eagles poised at either side of the proscenium arch. The little points of light danced on the red velvet curtains of the boxes, fluttered across the dark plush of the fat seats, flicked little tongues of triumph at Tom Maguire and his pink Jenny Lind.

Yankee Robinson's opening night in this masterpiece of wedding-cake architecture registered itself in big red letters as the night Mrs. Stark brought down the house.

Mrs. Kirby-Wingate-Stark was not by her best friends characterized as a delicate, pale dove of the footlights. She was more on the brooding pouter-pigeon order, and she took herself and her Art very seriously. She stepped forward that night beneath the glitter and glory and solemnly delivered herself of the weighty ode Dr. Robinson had composed for the occasion:

> Could we tonight the eternal slumbers break
> Of Avon's Bard, and bid the dreamer wake,
> The astonished muse would bid the poet turn,
> And sleep again beneath the honored urn. . . .

The Bard was listening and took the hint: the entire theater shivered, groaned, and sank two inches.

This caused a great stir and flutter in the audience, but everybody kept his seat. Rumor, that had originally held the building to be unsafe, now in the absence of tragic results proclaimed it merely unstable. Shakespeare and Sheridan went back to sleep, and the American Theater balanced well enough on the uneasy sands.

Although off to a shaky start, the Doctor steadied himself and plunged into a managerial duel with Napoleon Tom. First he cut prices. This forced the Jenny Lind to the inevitable counterblow, a price slash of her own. The result was to lure closer to the contest an uninvited kibitzer who managed to ruin both battlers periodically: the high cost of running a theater. This high cost factor—actors' salaries, bills for the building, expenses of all kinds—won more rounds in the long run than either of the star rivals.

Stock companies all over the United States had smelled gold by the beginning of 1852 and were streaming into San Francisco. Tom and the Doctor used them as pawns in the battle. The Doctor had, of course, an invaluable rook in the property of Yankee Robinson, creator as well as star actor in farces that had limitless miner-appeal. And he had sturdy king and queen pieces in the powerful Starks. Tom countered with a queen of his own: Mrs. Alexina Baker. Where Mrs.

Stark was a blood-and-thunder empress, Mrs. Baker specialized in being a regal lady, simple, sweet and charming, exactly the type to make the wifeless ones dream of the girls they left behind. She and her husband also thought it was not beneath the dignity of a stock company to do a little rehearsing: they were thus able to grace the Jenny Lind with finished, workmanlike productions and draw Tom a full house without benefit of tricks and novelties.

Tom also had a valuable bishop: Junius Booth, Jr., (known as June), oldest son of the great tragedian. Young Booth came to California early in 1852, and became Tom's manager. Though unimportant as an actor, as ruler over the performances of other actors "June" Booth was one of the best in the country.

In October, 1851, right on cue, the Chapman family blew into town in time to help Mrs. Stark sink the American on opening night. The Chapmans were a close-knit clan of troupers, said to be originators of the first Mississippi showboat. During the managerial struggle of early 1852, Tom and the Doctor went through a considerable tug of war over the Chapmans, who consented to honor first one theater and then the other with their lively and popular services, but who belonged to themselves and nobody else. Caroline and her brother Billy Chapman cut themselves big golden slices of the California pie all during the kaleidoscopic fifties.

Both theaters drew full houses all spring. But no matter how good the box office was, everything cost so much and actresses notoriously lived high. By June, 1852, Tom Maguire was in trouble: all his creditors wanted cash, and Tom didn't have any. He merely had friends on the city's Board of Aldermen. So Tom evaded bankruptcy by selling his third Jenny Lind to the City of San Francisco, to be used as a City Hall.

A great many citizens were very much surprised to find they had bought the gambler's theater for their new City Hall and were not sure they would have bought it if they had known in advance that they were going to do so. But the deal was made, and the asking price of two hundred thousand dollars was in Tom's hands, and the city fathers were packing their boxes and moving to their fancy new home.

By this rapid maneuver, Tom Maguire had escaped the financial squeeze; now it was Yankee Robinson's turn for trouble. Trouble didn't corner the fast-moving Doctor until the end of that year, and at that had a big assist from the eternal jinx, Mrs. Stark.

On Hallowe'en night of 1852, one year after the American Theater's shaky beginning, the Starks were playing in a melodrama called *The Stranger*. This typical heart-wringing production required in one scene the services of a small boy. The small boy had only to come on stage and be swept up into the grateful arms of his palpitating mother who had just been tearing large handfuls of false hair from her head because he was forever gone from her. Naturally, Yankee Robinson didn't intend to pay some urchin to endure Mrs. Stark's maternal embrace when he had a small son of his own. Little did he know it would have paid him many times over to engage for that famous bit almost anybody else but his son Charles.

At the appointed hour, austere and long-suffering Mrs. Robinson routed Charles from his bed and brought him down to the theater. Charles was stuffed into a red suit and pushed, rubbing his eyes, frantic with sleepiness, out upon the American's stage. He opened his eyes just wide enough to see a huge dark shape bearing down upon him with loud cries of "My son, my son!" He was not her son, but he knew who she was, for he had heard his father speak of her in the privacy of their home. Unfortunately he repeated exactly the words his father had said—and he knew the tone of voice, too—but they cannot be repeated here because, being by Victorian standards unprintable, they failed to get into the record.

Mrs. Stark, greeted in this unfilial style by the son of her manager, could never prove Charles learned his unfriendly comment at his father's knee, but she had her suspicions. Professional relations between the Starks and the Doctor exploded in a great uproar of name-calling, and the Starks trooped indignantly over to Tom's place. Tom at once showed proper appreciation of genius by allowing Mr. Stark to play King Lear for his first benefit.

Charles Robinson appeared once more on the boards of the American, two months after his Hallowe'en trick. At the end of December he helped his bankrupt father close shop: dressed in the memorable red suit, he contributed to the Farewell Performance a chirping rendition of his father's song, "Nary a Red, Nary a Red," which phrase translated roughly: flat, dead broke.

Assisted by Charles and Mrs. Stark, Robinson was now out of the battle and Tom was doing fine. With the money San Francisco gave him for his Jenny Lind, Tom had erected a less ambitious "Temple of the Muses," the San Francisco Hall. His opening overlapped the Doctor's farewell by a few days; on Christmas Day, 1852, he flashed his new queen before the eyes of the public when he introduced the first of the big-money prima donnas, Elisa Biscaccianti, from his stage.

Tom held more than the queen. He held the ace of the American stage also, and though that ace slipped through his fingers very quickly, the mere fact that he had played it gave Tom added prestige.

Early in the summer of 1852, when Maguire struggled in financial quicksands and theatricals dosed in dull siesta after a bright spring of divas, comics, and melodrama artists, a man with a commanding bearing and a dark and brilliant face strode off the ship and through the streets of San Francisco. Close to him, a little behind him, walked a melancholy anxious youngster, his inseparable companion and sometime caretaker. Junius Brutus Booth Sr., greatest tragedian of his time, and his obscure son Edwin had finally listened to the urging of June Booth and sailed to California.

Booth was at this time at the height of his triumph and not far from the end of his turbulent, glorious life. Edwin—shy, awkward, moody—destined to be the innovator of a natural untheatrical acting style which seemed like no acting at all to his declamatory father—was then no more than a shadowed and unimportant boy.

Although Tom Maguire had already made his deal with the city fathers, he held onto the Jenny Lind long enough to give the tragedian a suitable stage and win for himself the honor of presenting San Francisco with its first real star. For two weeks, flanked by his sons and supported by the Chapmans, Booth played Hamlet, Richard III, Othello, and the other major roles which he had so molded that no other actor of the time could play them without taking Booth's interpretation into account. Into these roles, which fit his own tortured and neurotic personality like a second skin, Booth poured the bitterness and madness and genius that had made him a legend. Excitement ran like an electric current through the waning season, as San Franciscans sat fascinated and awe-stricken in the Jenny Lind's galleries, watching every powerful gesture, listening to every impassioned word of that deep and magical voice.

San Francisco, even in 1852, was ripe for Booth. Sacramento was not. The Booths toured the interior with distressing results. The flannel-shirt boys knew tragedy at first hand—they knew it in terms of drowned partners, snow and starvation, careless shooting and struggles with the suicide urge. They looked coldly upon the posturing, declamatory style of tragic acting, the manner of that period which

108

Booth personified and brought to final fruition. Either they were too unsophisticated for Art, or they were too wise in the ways of harsh reality, too close to life, ever to return to that point of remoteness from ugly truth which that kind of sophistication requires.

The Booths returned to San Francisco, where the great tragedian, thoroughly embittered, played a week's engagement and sailed away. His sons remained behind, June to manage Tom Maguire's new San Francisco Hall, Edwin to endure a fiery tempering process in the westernmost of "the provinces." They never saw their father again.

With June Booth to manage his theater and the Chapmans to romp through popular comedies, Napoleon Tom held all the cards. He used them to add another star to his galaxy: Yankee Robinson.

Making the offer in a way that implied the Doctor would be doing Tom a big favor to help him out, Maguire gave his defeated opponent a stage for his skits and songs, finished him off as a rival operator, bought himself a paying property (Robinson was still very popular) and won himself a reputation for handsome generosity to a defeated competitor.

It was hard for Yankee Robinson to recite lines others had written, which he now had to do when the company was short of routine actors for stock parts. But in return for this hack work, he was allowed full play for his forte, the topical songs and satirical skits which he and the miners loved. Robinson and the Chapmans turned the San Francisco Hall into a gay frolicking madhouse night after night; the customers loved it and expressed their appreciation in cash, and Tom was happy. Tom was also very busy getting control of theaters here and there all over the state, creating a network, building an empire which would flower in later decades.

Dazed and brooding, completely out of time with this zany crew, Edwin Booth waited meekly for his managerial brother to give him

109

jobs to do. June gladly obliged: Edwin Booth, destined to be the greatest Hamlet of his day, played the lead part "Mose"—crudest and stupidest of comic stage fireboys—in the tawdry farce hit of the decade, *The American Fireman.*

If this atypical casting outrages the hearts of those who know American theater, the fate of young Edwin in the mining camps would harrow them still more. All the stars of San Francisco regularly "toured the interior." But they were not all greeted in the same way.

The potential genius of young Hamlet struck no answering spark from the gold hunters. Almost anyone could do better—if she was a woman. What drew the men pell-mell from their camps and huts was the chance to look at golden curls and cerulean blue eyes, the chance to listen to the warbling of a spine-tingling soprano voice.

When it came to prospecting, the thespians who struck it rich were not actors like Booth, but beautiful prima donnas like Elisa Biscaccianti and that graceful Swan of Erin, Kate Hayes.

CHAPTER *10*

The Canyon Circuit

IN THE SPRING OF 1852, A PETITE AND RADIANT ITALIAN GIRL WITH A
VOICE GOLDEN AS EL DORADO'S NUGGETS CAME SAILING INTO SAN FRAN-
cisco. In the air all around her—that windy, wet air from the salt
flats of the Bay—was something like a charge of electricity looking
for a lightning rod: the great restless woman-hunger of the Argonauts.
They were ready to worship a goddess, and they had no goddess. Elisa
appeared to them like a vision on the stage of the American theater
that March. Elisa sang opera and "Home Sweet Home" to them like an
angel fresh from the heavenly choir, and the Argonaut bowed down to
the first of his goddesses.

Elisa apparently had an electrical effect on San Francisco
women, too. The few ladies in town—spoiled creatures—previously
had refused to dress up and glitter in the audience because the streets
were so muddy and the citizens so crude. Elisa's effect on the men put
new life in them: they decided it was worth while after all to buy a
new ball gown and decorate public affairs with their shining presence.
The spring of Biscaccianti brought more than the crocus to blossom in
the streets of the city.

Though this "Musical Columbus of the Pacific" made San Francisco her base for the year she stayed, she gave in to urgent requests
from her public and made a triumphal march through Sacramento,
Marysville, and all the clamoring villages of the great inland valleys.

But in spite of superior voice and training, she did not rake in the nuggets like her successor in the goddess business, Kate Hayes.

Elisa sat thoughtfully through Kate's first concert at the American in November, 1852. She applauded politely, but she knew a battle when she saw one coming up. Elisa moved over to Tom's theater, helping add glitter to the opening of the San Francisco Hall at Christmas. For a few months—until February, 1853—she tried to sing Kate down. Kate was, after all, nothing but a mediocre ballad singer with a beautiful Irish madonna face, a dreamy graceful walk, and a shrewd manager. Who was she to dethrone an established goddess?

But if Columbus was first, people did not therefore honor him when they named the new world; and if Elisa was first, she nevertheless had failed to locate the claim where the great big ones were buried.

The Swan of Erin found it all right: her press agent, like Yankee Robinson, had an angle. He saw to it that Kate went in heavily for being the darling of the Volunteer Fire Companies and for auctioning concert tickets to the highest bidder.

Redheaded Kate called herself a soprano prima donna. The quality of her voice comes negatively reflected to us in typical newspaper praise: "A glance at her person assures us that she is a woman of extraordinary genius." A glance from a woman-starved Argonaut —not even a listen—was all Kate Hayes needed to bring into operation her extraordinary genius for removing nuggets from money belts.

In nothing else did the forty-niner express his special feeling for absent Woman—a feeling part chivalry, part hunger, part awe that such fabulous creatures really did exist—more clearly than in the deification of Kate Hayes.

George Green, a butcher and chief of a San Francisco volunteer fire company, was a typical Hayes fan. He and his company attended her opening concert decked out in full dress—red woollen frock coats and blue trousers. By the time Kate was giving her third concert, her press agent had already hit on the scheme of auctioning off the best seats in the house (those nearest to Kate) to the highest bidder. George Green kept right on bidding until he woke up to find he had bought the number one location for the sum of $1125.

What was meat selling for?

The market value of auburn hair and "cerulean" eyes fluctuated rapidly in the next few months. Sam Brannan took a turn on the sucker list, to the tune of $625 for the prize position. The price trailed down to a mere $100 at the seventh concert (Green, a fiend for punishment, back again). In 1853 the Sutter Rifles bid the "best seat" up to an all-time Hayes high of $1200. They presented this treasure to Captain John Sutter, who spent the evening feasting his eyes from a green sofa right next to the stage. Anybody would think that the Swan's voice (an odd nickname, since swans have no voice except when dying) didn't have much carrying power beyond the first row.

Kate Hayes had intended to leave California fairly soon, but she couldn't bring herself to go. She loved her miners too much. All during 1853 bouquets kept raining onto the stage as she finished her songs. These floral tributes were coy hiding places for anything from a fifty-dollar slug to a diamond brooch.

But Kate lingered too long. Reaction set in. Everyone gasped when newspapers broke the news that her coachman was suing her for twelve hundred dollars back pay. After all, she took in that much, once, for a single ticket.

Hurriedly Kate Hayes announced a farewell concert (the first of several, for she was an incorrigible stage-doorway-stander) in May, and sailed away leaving the easy money for somebody else.

Somebody else turned out to be an unknown American singer,

Ella Bruce. The Marysville No. 1 Hook and Ladder Company belligerently rang the cash registers for Ella's concert to the tune of seventeen hundred dollars for best seat, and settled back with patriotic satisfaction to gloat:

Ella was no foreign gold digger, but one of their very own, American edition.

In the days when Kate Hayes and her rival goddesses prospected so successfully, and the Booths so poorly, "barnstorming the interior" usually meant touring Sacramento, Stockton, Marysville—at the worst, some of the big prosperous camps like Hangtown and Nevada City. It was in Nevada City in December, 1852, that Edwin Booth—climaxing weeks of apathetic audiences, unsuitable hack roles, threadbare box-office receipts which hardly allowed the cast eating money—huddled like a miserable puppy, snowbound and dead broke. When finally the mail got through the drifts, it brought him the news that his father was dead. Junius Brutus Booth, Sr., had died alone, unattended, on a Mississippi riverboat.

"Absent thee from felicity awhile?" No, Hamlet was not even allowed a time to mourn; at once he had to join a party of desperate characters who preferred freezing in the open to starving in the town. They organized and struck out over the mountain snow. Edwin fought through the drifts with them to Marysville, and from there downtrail to civilization, to bring the news to June in San Francisco. June had heard it. All June could offer was work—the job at the San Francisco Hall—and Hamlet, bewildered and sickened by his loss, defeated in his first bout with the mountain circuit, settled down to play the broad-comedy fireboy, Mose.

But while Booth had a bad time in the diggings, both then and later, it was not an easy route even for the goddesses, even for the skylarks. The stages jolted through the muddy ruts; the mining camps

114

offered poor fare and outrageous beds; the pampered darlings had to "rough it" if they went after the gold in its native habitat. Most of them couldn't take it. The customers could pay, all right—and did pay, when they got what they wanted. But the gold diggers behind the smoky whale-oil footlights (and it gives one satisfaction to note it) had to put their backs into it in order to extract those nuggets.

Sometimes it was worse than that. The acting team of Mr. and Mrs. Eldridge were walking down the streets of Hangtown, minding their own business, when a man lurched out of a saloon, saw before his twice-dazed eyes a lovely lady, and got wildly enthusiastic. Eldridge seized the man, as any gentlemanly husband would do—but the barfly bristled with the usual arsenal, and Eldridge was unarmed. Mrs. Eldridge rushed home for a pistol (apparently all action stopped while she did this) and returned in time to shoot her annoyer. At least she shot at him; in the natural excitement of the moment, she missed. Nevertheless it was a good try, and it smoothed the way considerably for later actresses who played in Hangtown.

In the early years of the rush, the boys who didn't get to town very often were on a low-calorie diet when it came to fun and games. They had their club—there was always some kind of a tent in the neighborhood for the monte tables—but the flashy ladies didn't penetrate any farther uphill than they had to, they stopped when they got to a good stopping place, and public amusements of any kind were scarcer than gold dust in the waters under the Golden Gate. Between the wilderness of the high Sierra diggings and the rough civilization of valley and foothill towns, snow drifted deep in winter. No wagon road led from Red Dog to You Bet, no stage ran, and sometimes even a jackass couldn't get through.

So while the valley towns enjoyed from the first the backwash of San Francisco's burgeoning show business, the early theater of the mining camps was forced by necessity into a different mold. Among the isolated prospectors, mediocre backwoods fiddlers, strolling guitarists, harrowing musical amateurs and all such driftwood of the music halls found an easily satisfied audience. Any curly headed miner's child who could lisp a few verses of a Jim Crow song was lionized as a prodigy and showered with gold dust. These became a special breed, sentimentally entitled "Fairy Stars."

Miners left their poker game, abandoned their chuck-a-luck dice and clustered into the saloon doors, watching with avid curiosity while a queer little gnome of a man rode slowly down the canyon street on a sleepy donkey, ringing a bell and announcing in town-crier tones: "D. V. Gates will have the honor of giving an oratorical and theatrical performance." And who was D. V. Gates? Why, the man on the donkey. "I 'caved,' " wrote a bystander, telling the people at home of his amazement when he learned that this wizened creature planned to show the town a big time all by himself.

Gates could, and did. He rang his own bell, "posted his own bills, beat his own drum, fiddled, sang, danced, and recited, and gave a ball after the dramatic performance." He could do imitations of Henry Clay, Daniel Webster and other noted figures; he could present farcical skits, deliver monologues, or help out a shorthanded stock company with a quick fill-in performance as the dark hero of *Othello*. When he wasn't being a thespian of all work, he was part of various regular troupes; he was one of the people snowed-in with Edwin Booth in Nevada City.

As an entertainer, Gates came from a drawer quite a bit down from the top. But he was playing towns deprived for many weeks of any show more novel than a gun battle or a hanging. His boast was that nobody ever took him up on the money-back guarantee he habitually offered.

Lacking even a D. V. Gates, the miners had to improvise. Mokelumne Hill boasted its very own stock company, known as Clark's. Clark, a clerk for Adams Express Company, rented a building and rounded up companions to help him turn it into a theater. They painted backdrops, sewed old rags together for curtains, and invented a curious footlight gimmick: candles set at intervals along a board that stretched full length beneath the stage front, with holes in the stage above it. At the prompter's desk was a lever which raised the candles when the script said "Daylight," or lowered them when a romantic gloom was in order.

Romantic gloom was definitely in order for love scenes, as Clark's Mokelumne Hill Company was an all-male organization. There were two good reasons for this. "One was that we gave the pure drama as it was given at the time of Queen Elizabeth, when such a thing as a female actress was unknown," explained a participant. The other reason was that there wasn't an English-speaking female in town.

An all-local-talent outfit entertained at Craycroft's American Theater, in Downieville. Downieville writers supplied an occasional opus, passionately local, like *Heloi, or the Robbers of the Sierra Nevada,* a hair-raiser guaranteed to make the toughest prospector peek under his cot for Joaquin Murietta. The Downieville amateurs danced hornpipes, sang nautical songs, and put on a burlesque of *Macbeth.* Sometimes the program included a wandering Chinese juggler, and "SPARRING . . . By a couple of the Fancy," which meant that a pair of corner-saloon prospectors could flail at each other onstage instead of on street, and get paid.

But Craycroft had neglected something: his playhouse wasn't winterproof. The *Mountain Echo* lamented:

FALL OF THE DRAMA—IN DOWNIEVILLE.—Heaviest performance of the season—last act of the snow king of the mountains—on Christmas night we heard a tremendous crash, and on going to find the cause, saw our beautiful theater a complete ruin. The roof fell in from the weight of the snow; and demolished everything in its descent.

The roof didn't happen to fall in on anybody; and the thespians that the roof should have fallen in on rarely supported any blow heavier than the quick-healing bruise from a hard-flung scrap of gold.

Of women who endured this kind of occupational hazard, Kate Hayes and Biscaccianti were exceptions, in that they were famous and they could sing—even Kate could sing, in comparison with her competition. The girls didn't really have to sing. They only had to get up on a stage and look beautiful, and mouth sentimental ballads, and catch the gold as it came their way.

A wandering warbler in Downieville struck pay dirt in the heart of John Kelly to the extent of a hundred-dollar nugget. The rest of the boys presented her with a five-hundred-dollar chain of fine gold specimens. But as the gift without the giver is bare, they re-emphasized their love by risking pneumonia the night she left in order to serenade her: "The rain came down in torrents; but this did not serve to cool the ardor of a score of love-sick swains, who stood in the mud to their knees singing up at her window, 'Open thy lattice to me, love.' "

There is no record that she opened her lattice the least little bit on this occasion. But there are many dark hints in the Jeremiah articles written by the pious that this California custom of overwhelming Beauty with Gold put quite a strain on the high moral principles of Beauty.

In the later fifties, improved roads and a market flooded with entertainers gave the mountain circuit a greater abundance and a wider variety of entertainment. The miners could afford to be choosy then. They even gave a temporary home to that greatest of contemporary glamour girls, Lola Montez, when she was permanently retired from her job as Bavarian King Louis's mistress and almost permanently retired from the job of pretending to be an actress.

But before 1854, it was a case of make over and make do, and make an extravagant drunken uproar over any showman and especially any showgirl who came their way.

However, while the theater of prima donnas and dancing stars was a rare and longed-for dream on the verge of becoming real, the arena of cruelty and death was a present reality in many of the camps. A womanless culture, though open to the potentially civilizing influence of the theater, was still more vulnerable to the decivilizing lure of commercialized sadism, the arena. Soon, as the stage rose to prominence, the arena would sink out of sight.

In the opening fifties, this change had not taken place: the death sport stood on the cliff edge of its popularity, on top of the world, not yet pushed over into the plunge to oblivion. What the fun-loving American boys of the mines could not take out in serenading sopranos, they took out in screaming for the blood of bull or bear or luckless Mexican toreador.

CHAPTER *11*

Roman Holiday

INTO A MAKESHIFT ARENA OF STICKS AND UNDERBRUSH STEPPED A
SLENDER DARK GIRL IN A RAGGED AND GLITTERING COSTUME. THE
miners on the rough benches fell silent as she stood there waiting, a
señorita scarcely out of her teens, brave in the tattered regimentals of
old Spain.

Trembling in the center of the ring stood the bony range bull
who had just killed a picador's horse and exhausted five or six Mexicans. The girl approached. Sword in hand, she fenced with him, swaying gracefully out of reach when he dashed at her, pricking his flank
as he pounded past until each rush left behind it a spattering trail of
red.

Turning, plunging furiously, he bore down on his tormentor.
She, graceful as a dancer and strong armed as a warrior, thrust the
sword into his body up to the hilt. The twist of her wrist and the on-
ward lunge of the bull drove the sword death-deep into him and he
fell shuddering, his blood spraying hot and bright over the glistening
jacket of the killer.

Silver dollars, nuggets and flowers rained down into the pit. The
lady bowed, picked up her golden pay check, and retired as quietly as
she had entered.

Bullfights were never like this in Spain. Bullfights were hardly
ever like this in California.

You could no more tell what kind of fare you'd get at the arena

120

from reading the advertising bills than you could gamble on curing your broken leg because the wrapper on the medicine bottle claimed one drink would knit crushed bones.

Before one such sporting event, handbills announced all over town that the celebrated Señorita Ramona Perez would duel with the bull. This proved to be more bull than señorita: when the miners flocked to watch Ramona perform, the matador who entered the ring was "very well got up as a woman, with the slight exception of a very fine pair of mustaches, which he had not thought it worth while to sacrifice. He had a fan in his hand, with which he half concealed his face, as if from modesty, as he curtsied to the audience, who received him with shouts of laughter—mixed with hisses and curses, however, for there were some who had been true believers in the senorita. . . . The senorita played with the bull for some little time with the utmost of feminine grace, whisking her petticoats in the bull's face with one hand, whilst she smoothed down her hair with the other." At last she daintily dug the sword into the back of the bull's neck, dropped sword and red flag, and "ran out of the arena, curtsying, and kissing her hand to the spectators, after the manner of a ballet-dancer leaving the stage."

The role of female impersonators in gold-country culture comes to us only in casual asides like this. We know men dressed as women on the stage sometimes—Robinson's partner, Evrard, was a well-known female impersonator in the theater. We know men were designated to be the "ladies" at all-male fandangoes—but the references were all completely innocent, insubstantial as San Francisco fog. There is nothing solid enough to analyze in the records left by an age that paid to watch animals and men kill, tolerated shooting battles, supported the miserable Chinese prostitute of the slums—but would have hanged Dr. Kinsey from the nearest oak.

The Argonaut's love of a joke, and the sometime crudity and morbidity of his wit, is better documented. The boundary between cruelty and humor was blurred to the vanishing point: he burlesqued everything, even death. The man flouncing prettily about the ring was comic in the extreme; the miner's disappointment in finding no señorita he took as a good joke on himself; and to top his pleasure, he could witness the killing of an animal. It added up to a satisfying afternoon.

In Spain the bullfight was a romantic remnant of medieval glory. The poor relation of the bullfight that migrated to Spanish California via Mexico arrived diminished and bedraggled by the journey. Usually the bulls were no magnificent Andalusian beasts born and bred for the ring, but dreary range cattle intended for the hide-and-tallow trade. The toreadors were occasionally competent professionals from Mexico, but more often amateurs, idle Mexican boys with an itch for exhibitionism and a need for monte money.

The arenas varied from heavy wooden structures in the cities to flimsy tottering things of brush and sticks in the mines. The edges of a good arena's pit were planked up about twenty feet; tiers of benches rose from the top of this planking, and at one side was a door raised by pulleys. In the villages, the pit had a board fence around the fighting area, a canvas wall ten feet in back of it, and a brush wall behind that. Between brush and canvas the miners stood to watch, protected by nothing more solid than the wooden fence and the no man's land between it and the canvas. This at least added a sporting element to the spectator's role.

Bullfighting was one public amusement the gringos found ready-made and waiting when they arrived in '49. Miners herded out to the Mission Dolores, near San Francisco, to mingle with the natives and watch fascinated and sometimes shamefaced while a swarthy fellow whacked away at a tough little beast. Like wide-open gambling, this was an exotic pastime of foreigners which they, free from Anglo-Saxon civilization, could now enjoy. And they could do so without feeling in the least responsible. What could you expect of a pack of crazy heathens? But increasingly the gory incidents of the ring fed an appetite for blood the forty-niner never knew he had.

In the regulation bullfights, men were rarely killed outright. (Horses were not so lucky.) The semitrained units from Mexico, which operated in the city shows, were quite capable of performing their historic roles: first scratching the animal from horseback with spears, then trimming him up with a bright collar of red rosettes stuck into his shoulders on cruel little spikes, and at last retiring politely out of the way. "Your dance, toreador—" and the star of the afternoon strutted arrogantly in to finish off the maddened and blinded creature.

The forty-niner cheered for the bull.

Once in a while the bull won. Some dark little cow-hand's son, intoxicated by the dream of the red cloak, would slip unannounced into the ring. When this happened the miners often got more than their money's worth: human bloodshed, even human death.

It was not because a Mexican boy or a fine horse lost his life occasionally that the Argonauts turned from bullfights to other torture shows. Partly they grew bored with the bullfight when the novelty wore off, and began to demand a new outlet for the appetite it had aroused. Partly they lived in too many places where the supply of regular matadors and eager Mexican boys was inadequate and they developed no toreadors among themselves.

So they had to look for other exhibitions to satisfy the deep thread

123

of cruelty that runs hidden in all men and comes to the surface when wars or frontier conditions slacken the pressure of social decency and hypocrisy.

The Mexicans, sensing the shift, were anxious to hold their nugget-happy customers. In the effort to do so they incorporated some of the tricks and comedy of the circus. Blindfolded bullfighters on horseback burlesqued the proud toreador. A clown stood on the shoulders of the matador to plant the gay little flags of cruelty between the horns of the plunging beast. One day a certain Señor Nicholas advertised that he intended to "jump over a bull while furiously rushing at him," which must have required superior powers of co-ordination.

The Americans were not much impressed. For variety, they turned to the bull-and-bear fight.

California was particularly well suited to this kind of contest, for the grizzlies who prowled Sierra forests were the only bears fierce enough to match a bull. (When some sharper tried to pass off a poor little black bear as a grizzly, the results were deplorable.) Bear-catching became big business. All over the state men made a fine profit by capturing the savage creature in traps, in pits, or with many lassos thrown from several directions at once to confuse the bear and, drawn taut while the horses dug in, to hold him snarling helplessly, a giant bumblebee in a web. The bear-catchers then confined their bear in an iron cage and sold him for prices ranging up to $2000 to the bull-and-bear promoters of the nearest town.

There were two drawbacks to this sport. One was that bull and bear, impelled by their own native wisdom, wished nothing better than to give each other the widest possible berth. Another was that the bull generally tended to have the best of it.

From these circumstances grew an elaborate but variable system

124

of house rules. Sometimes men chained the bear to a ring in the middle of the arena, giving the bull freedom of the pit. (For obvious reasons, the grizzly could never have freedom of the pit, unless he won it by breaking the chain.) As this gave the bull an unfair advantage, most promoters tied bull and bear together with a short length of cable (or tied both of them to the ring), figuring familiarity would soon breed contempt.

Preparing the animals in this way took great skill. If the bull entered first, he was teased by picadors, lassoed, thrown down and held, and the iron chain fastened to one hind leg. Then the hard-working attendants lifted the trap door of the bear's cage just enough to grasp one paw with a pair of tongs, draw it out and secure it with the other end of the chain. The bear was ready to be released. If the grizzly was known to be a bull-killer on the basis of his record, the other method—leaving the bull free—might apply.

The boys that did this job lived dangerously. Watching them work was one of the extra thrills for the audience at the bull-and-bear fight.

General Scott, most formidable of ursine toreadors, "made his appearance before the public in a very bearish manner." The attendants pushed his cage into the ring on wheels and established the chain in such a manner that the General was allowed to come within a foot or two of the fence. Then "the General was rolled out upon the ground all of a heap, and very much against his inclination apparently, for he made violent efforts to regain his cage as it disappeared. When he saw that was hopeless, he floundered half-way round the ring at the length of his chain, and commenced to tear up the earth with his fore-paws." He proceeded to scrape a hole in the earth for himself and lie down in it, which was his customary fighting attitude and a good one, judging by his record for killing bulls. In this position he could do tremendous damage with paws and jaws to the bull thundering past or over him.

These sporting events became common and very popular. When Sacramento's Colonel Price staged a fight at Brighton in which one giant bear faced three bulls, the paper boasted that with such brave attractions Brighton must "become even more than ever the resort of the gay and fashionable who seek recreation and amusement in a ride out of town."

When the gay and fashionable could manage to make bull and bear join in combat, the battle was many times bloodier than a bull-fight. The bear never heard of Castilian etiquette of the ring. He went in for nose chewing and rib cracking. If he got a death grip on the bull's tongue—his favorite hold—he was champion; but if the bull, with greater freedom to wield horns like curved daggers, could get in the first blow, he gored his enemy to death before the grizzly could get started. The bear's thick fur made this single lethal stab difficult, and more often than not the fight ended with both creatures so mutilated that both had to be shot.

There were other problems. When promoters chained bull and bear together, both beasts were cramped: the bull lacked room to make his deadly rushes, and the bear found it difficult to bring his huge body into action or utilize his greatest asset, tremendous weight —usually estimated at over a thousand pounds. But all problems are soluble while the box office is in healthy condition.

Sometimes the customers got more blood than they had paid for. William Perkins recorded a bull-and-bear fight to end all bull-and-bear fights—which he hoped the authorities would be shocked enough to do, after assessing the cost of this particular day's work.

This "novel amusement" came to Sonora late in 1851. Perkins considered it "quite in keeping with the wild or half civilized state we

126

are in and the rough semi-savage propensities of our population."
Before an audience of more than two thousand, the bear—secured to
a central ring by a ten-foot chain—faced three bulls at once. The bulls
and the bear gave each other a few minor wounds, but in the process
the whole bull team got frightened, fought shy and had to be removed
in disgrace.

Then, having let the three Ferdinands handle the preliminary
softening-up process, promoters introduced a splendid black bull,
proud and quivering with rage. This bull bounded about, pawed the
dirt, bellowed ferociously in approved bull style. He saw the bear;
he appropriately hated the bear, and immediately lunged for him.

> Master Bruin curled himself up into a ball and the
> furious bull rushed over him, missing his stroke. The bear
> with wonderful quickness sprang up at this moment and
> caught the bull by the thigh with his teeth, inflicting a
> ghastly wound. The noble animal gave a roar of mingled
> agony and rage, turned round and catching his adversary
> with his tremendous horns, raised him, notwithstanding his
> enormous weight, and made him perform a somerset that
> was bounded by the length of the chain. The bear fell with
> a shock that seemed sufficient to break every bone in his
> body; but no; quick as a flash he had again given the bull a
> severe wound in the haunch and the latter moved off to a
> little distance to breathe. In a few moments he again made a
> gallant attack, again gave the bear a tremendous goring and
> was again driven off by the frightful wound he received
> from the teeth of the Grizzly who appeared to keep his
> temper better than his antagonist and consequently fought
> under greater advantage.
> Four times did the brave brute make a desperate attack
> and, although the bear was badly hurt, the bull always got
> the worst of it, until cowed and scared by a last fearful bite,
> when the bear caught him by the head, he turned and collect-
> ing all his remaining strength, with one bound he topped
> the palisades and dropped like something more than a hot

potato amongst a crowd of Mexicans. The terror was intense; such a scampering! such an outcry!

Several people were badly hurt and one was gored to death by the infuriated animal.

Having lacerated the grizzly, wounded several men and killed one, the bull took to the hills until pursuing horsemen ran him down and lassoed him. But the show wasn't over. In the center of the ring the champion lay exhausted and panting. A Mexican came up to him with a bucket of water to pour over him and, thinking the bear was at the end of his rope both figuratively and literally, walked too close. The bear sprang up, caught the man in his arms, threw him down and closed his jaws over the man's thigh, crushing it "as if it were a willow stick. We distinctly heard the snapping of the brute's teeth as they closed through the flesh and bone. . . .

Then followed a scene that could only have taken place in California. . . . The man was under the bear and the beast was crunching his leg with his teeth. In an instant a score of revolvers were drawn and fired. The bear was riddled with balls and the man was untouched! The most fatal shot was in the bear's head, and this proceeded from a man standing above the crowd on the topmost bench; and he fired over the heads of two or three hundred people. At least, this person claims the honor of having sent a ball within a few inches of the Mexican's body into the bear's head.

The sharpshooter did not rescue the Mexican from his death, but merely delayed it; the amputation of his leg, under surgical conditions then existent in Sonora, could not save him.

Death's box score on that afternoon included a couple of men as well as a couple of beasts, and even the Argonaut began to wonder if this wasn't carrying the blood lust a little too far.

This kind of accident, while it gave the thrill seekers pause, did not always result in tragedy. Sometimes it was sheer farce, the kind the forty-niner loved best.

One memorable afternoon a frightened bear fled from the snorting bull with such a tremendous thrust of his great weight that the chain broke. Moving like a ton of greased lightning, the bear took up a new position in the nearest oak tree. This tree happened to be bearing a heavy fruit of cheapskates who had found ringside perches for free by clinging to the overhanging branches. Their response to the invasion was a lesson in the swiftness of human reaction time. Some let go and plunged to earth, others slipped crashing and howling down the outer branches. In a matter of seconds, the bear had the tree all to himself.

A traveler wrote home: "It looked as if old Bruin had jumped into a pond and drive out all the frogs."

The bull-and-bear fight, like the bullfight, ran its course and began to decline. Danger to spectators may have caused this loss of interest, or it may have resulted mostly from the restlessness of the forty-niner. Faddish and fickle, he did not keep any one sport or famous entertainer buoyed up with his enthusiasm and gold for very long at a time. His entertainment taste ran not to stars but to skyrockets, or at best comets.

Promoters tried all kinds of new tricks in the animal-fighting field. They claimed the bear was no match for the bull, and found him new sparring mates: they set him against mountain lions, or against his small cousin the black bear. After a while they paired the grizzly with a jackass. This, of course, was just plain murder for the jackass.

Alfred Jackson wrote about one of these fights in Nevada City. The advertising poster proclaimed a battle between a ferocious grizzly and the champion fighting jackass of the state. The champion ass was supposed to have conquered two bulls and killed a mountain

129

lion in previous contests. When the customers—two thousand of them —got a look at the jackass, he "didn't show to whip a sick pup, let alone a fierce grizzly."

As soon as men turned the jackass loose, he started nibbling grass. Then they opened the bear's cage. The bear wouldn't come out. They poked the bear and prodded him. ". . . when he finally waddled into the enclosure there was a roar from the crowd that made the woods ring. Instead of a fierce, bloodthirsty grizzly it was only a scared little cinnamon bear that didn't weigh over four hundred or five hundred pounds." The bear sat quietly awhile, frightened by the noise. Finally he walked over towards the donkey. When he got near enough, the donkey let him have it with both feet and went on calmly eating grass. "The bear picked himself up, made a break for the fence, went over it in two jumps and started for the chapparal."

The crowd scattered, some of them shooting at the bear. The bear got away. Everybody began shouting, "Hang the promoters." But the promoters had also taken to the hills. There was nothing left but the burro. The crowd formed a procession with the donkey at the head and all paraded down to the saloons, banging away with pistols as they marched. The boys spent the rest of the day driving the burro into saloon after saloon, pledging him as security for drinks, then taking up a collection to redeem him.

Jackson concluded: "I told Pard about it and he remarked that as we could not make the jackass drink he was the only sensible one in the outfit."

The process of degrading the bullfight went on. The crowning innovation was a tribute to Yankee ingenuity. One brilliant manager conceived the idea of putting the grizzly into a closed pen full of large gray rats. These vermin crawled around in his fur and brought

130

the mighty bear to a state of impotent, frustrated fury which the on-lookers found a new high tide of comedy.

Here was progress—here was American "go-aheadativeness." It took the sharpers and the frontier roughs only a few years to tear the gilt braid and silver spurs from the bloody pageant of old Spain and twist it to melodrama, to butchery, finally to farce.

"The affair passed through all stages, from the heroic to the lowest," was the un-American comment of a European tourist, "and the Yankees mocked the dignity of the bear as they do that of a king."

A bear in a pitful of rats: to this was Spain's grim and glittering ritual reduced.

CHAPTER *12*

Puppy Dog's Tails and Hangman's Noose

Delight in cruelty was not confined to the crowd at the arena. there were commoner amusements, petty ones, that satisfied the same urge. Those who felt impelled to seek their pleasure in the misery, injury or death of others would probably have known the same need in any time or place; in a land socially disorganized, keyed to a constant febrile pitch of excitement and unrestrained by the conventions of home or loving demands of families, they had unaccustomed freedom to indulge this need.

When one of "the fancy" had a quiet moment between bouts with bottle, he knew a subtle trick or two for dodging boredom. He could always find a little dog and tie a piece of meat to its tail. This made the little dog extremely popular with all the big dogs in town. You could practically laugh yourself sick watching those dogs go after that meat, fighting for a chance at the little dog's tail, snatching him and flinging him yipping into the air.

In case you didn't have any meat, you could wander around looking for a couple of Mexicans encouraging a cockfight. There was an Irishman in San Francisco who had a regular cockpit, and tickets were only two bits. But there wasn't much of this. Dogfights were commoner. If you were in luck, you might read on a saloon wall a handbill announcing one of these sponsored dogfights. Owners matched

132

their dogs, set up stakes and goaded the animals to battle. Lots of gold changed hands when one of the animals lay dead.

If your dog was vanquished but not killed, you criticized his performance with a bullet through his head.

What if there wasn't even a dog in sight? A brief hunt through the right part of San Francisco would turn up a Chinaman or two, and many people thought a Chinaman was more fun than a dog. Not that you necessarily shot at them, unless you were drunk or irritated about something. It was simpler than that: you grabbed the heathen by his pigtail, drew your bowie knife and clopped off a big hunk of hair. The Chinaman wasn't in the least injured by this, actually, but to hear him squeal you'd think it wasn't his hair but his neck that got the knife. The joke, of course, was that the stupid infidel believed he couldn't get into heaven if he lost his precious pigtail.

Lacking a bowie knife, you could have a milder kind of fun— and express disapproval of his outlandish religion—by tying old bones to that silly queue of his.

While unquestionably many of the forty-niners went in for fights, sadistic diversions and practical jokes with a strong knife-edge of cruelty to them, the amount of noise these characters made gave the impression that they existed in larger numbers than they actually did. On the other side, there were practical jokes that might be crude from the standpoint of civilized wit, but were without malice; and there were public indignation meetings to punish cruelty that outraged even gold-country standards.

William Taylor, the evangelist, tells us: "There was a fellow at Smith's Flat, who, to gratify some secret brutal passion of his own, tied a chicken, and put it alive on the fire, and cooked it for his dinner." This was only a chicken, and a chicken's life isn't worth much in a country where a man got a dose of lead for calling somebody a scoundrel. But the meanness, the nasty perversity of this particular act aroused the miners. They called a meeting at once and gave the culprit fifteen minutes to leave town. He left and was never heard of in that neighborhood again.

Many of the jokes the prospectors played on each other were tame and childish. Men liked to place a flat stone upon the chimney top of a friend's cabin and linger next morning to watch that friend attempting to cook breakfast in a cloud of smoke. When a liquor-dazed partner couldn't find his looking glass, it was fun to give him a piece of brick, persuade him it was a mirror and watch him try to cut his hair by it.

There was a joking feud between an actor named Anderson and a town character named Syd. Anderson had come out on the short end of a recent prank and wanted to get even. One night he found all the boys, including Syd, sitting around the big sheet-iron stove in the gambling saloon, warming their feet.

> All at once the front door was violently opened and in rushed Anderson. . . . He was hatless, and, from all appearances, was in the full enjoyment of a full-fledged case of "jim jams." He stepped to the stove and with his foot kicked open the door, at the same time drawing from under his coat a large powder horn, which he threw into the stove, exclaiming:
> "Let's all go together, boys!"

The saloon emptied as if a giant hand had turned it upside down on the street. Syd disentangled himself from a pile of arms and legs and listened for the blast. But all he saw was Anderson smiling in the doorway, and all he heard was sarcastic wisecracks from his rival jokesmith.

This is not to deny that many forty-niners enjoyed a good fight

134

better than any joke. When rival groups of Chinese miners quarreled and went to war in a mountain ravine, the miners took sides and urged the warriors on. They provided weapons, wagered large sums on the outcome, and a few of them even enlisted. The rest gathered on a convenient hillside to watch and cheer. Nobody sold tickets and there were no card tricks. When at last guns actually were fired and a dozen victims lay flat on the pine needles, everyone was satisfied that the Chinese actually would fight; the show was over, peace was declared, and the audience went home.

The best fights were fights between men. These might be street brawls, which you could join if you happened to feel lucky and healthy that day. But if you didn't suffer a bullet or a broken nose, you were likely to suffer from the interference of old nervous-nellies like the man who wrote to the Downieville *Echo* proposing "the idea of making a large pen out back from town, and putting all the fighting stock in together some Sunday, and then let them take a general knock down, and if they all get bloody noses, no matter. But this street fighting is decidedly beastly, and then occasionally an innocent man gets a rap on the nose."

There was another kind of battle, more exclusive, more elite: the duel. Duels were illegal, but that didn't bother anyone. Newspapers carried announcements of impending duels several days in advance, giving full information as to time, place, weapons, contestants, and declared grievance. Some duelists sent out formal engraved invitations to their friends, but you didn't really need an invitation—everybody crashed the party as a general custom. One critic expressed this:

> That no price is mentioned for the sight seems the only thing that distinguishes the entertainment from a bull or bear fight. If two notable characters be announced to perform a duel, say at the mission, half the city flocks to the

place, and of course, the spectators are much disappointed should nobody be slain.

Great excitement heralded the duel between politician Dave Broderick and Judge J. Caleb Smith. In a letter to a newspaper the Judge had incontinently described Broderick as a liar, a scoundrel and a blackguard. Those were things you didn't call Dave Broderick. A dark moody giant of a man, a gold-rush politico with an irrational urge to power and an inexhaustible rage to release upon those who wounded his hypersensitive honor, Broderick was a man you insulted only after releasing your safety catch. Smith had figuratively checked his powder supply and released his safety catch before he wrote to the papers.

Friends of each antagonist arranged to follow the ruffled gentlemen about and prevent (or organize?) the expected trouble.

And behind the heroes, behind the bodyguard that shadowed the heroes, skulked four or five hundred spectators, patiently waiting and hoping.

Finally, at the corner of Sacramento and Front streets, the two trains met. Broderick challenged and Smith accepted in due form. Members of the bodyguard presented themselves as seconds, and seconds were chosen. Followed by eager fight fans, the duelists adjourned to Contra Costa where they shot it out at twelve paces with Colt's Navy revolvers. After the starting order to fire, they fired at random for six rounds. At the sixth round a shot drew blood. Thereupon the duelists bowed, shook hands, declared their honors satisfied, and everybody went home.

A few years later in a similar duel with Judge Terry, aroused partly over the Civil War issue in which Terry took the Southern side, Broderick wasn't so lucky. He got a splendid funeral.

Duels had their lighter side. In Nevada City two rival musicians—

one a fiddler, the other a vocalist—habitually stimulated their talents with alcohol. But as all entertainers know, one step too far into your cups and all the good work is undone. When the spirit was too much on them, Wentworth and Dan could not harmonize. Dan was sawing away one day when Wentworth felt the urge to sing, and, unable to outdo the strident fiddle, told Dan to "stop that squealing thing." One word led to another; interested bystanders moved in, and everybody stepped outside. The seconds provided the pistols and handed them to the principals; the word was given, and both fired.

Wentworth fell to the ground, covered with blood. Appalled, old Dan dashed over and began to cry over him: "Poor feller, he wa'n't fit to die." Wentworth, his honor stinging all over again, jumped to his feet demanding, *"Who* wa'n't fit to die?"

Fit or not, nobody died in that one: the boys had loaded one pistol with powder only, and the other with a cartridge of currant jelly.

In dueling, as in other sports, there were always quick-witted individuals who could commercialize the game to their own advantage. Dr. Natchez, on Clay Street in San Francisco, catered to the sporting element with a pistol gallery. Here was a place you could practice when you had an affair of honor coming up. Natchez knew all about guns and pistols, could give you any information you wanted, would listen to your story and prescribe the only remedy for your disease, "the application of Colt's revolver to the breast of the transgressor." With the true objectivity of the professional man, Dr. Natchez would then supply weapons for both sides—at a price.

But duels had their limitations as a spectator sport. Often somebody just got nicked in the shoulder and called it a day. A hanging, now—that was the real thing and no mistake. One mining-camp diarist, commenting on a hanging he had recently witnessed, gave

137

the opinion that this victim, though a scoundrel, was no worse than many another scoundrel—but the town had not had a hanging for months and was ripe for one. The actual number of hangings in the diggings is probably exaggerated, and usually the punishment fitted the crime according to the rough standards of the frontier. Mining camps had no adequate jails, and there was no way to cope with offenders except banishment, whipping and the noose. Usually the impromptu jury decided its cases fairly enough. But at least once, a man was hung for horse stealing much too quickly. The horses were found the next day, wandering loose in the mountains. Unquestionably hanging served a secondary purpose in addition to controlling ruffians. It functioned as a public bloodletting when the blood pressure of the mob reached dangerous heights.

After the hanging of Irish Dick in the Fall of '50, Syd—the victim of the mock-explosion joke—argued that these hangings were preposterous, and that the most villainous rascals in town were always first to shout "Hang him!" and pull on the ropes. The men pulling on the rope might just as well be on the other end of it. Why, if you were to run through the streets of the town with a man right behind you shouting "Hang him!" these loafers would pour out of the bar-room and hang you without ever asking a question. They would hang you just on general principles.

Syd's cynical statement started an argument in the saloon. To test the question, everyone agreed that this particular drama must be performed at once, and a young man volunteered to play hare to the hounds for the sake of experiment.

The young man started down the street at a brisk trot. His friends fell in behind him, screaming "Hang him!" Every bar emptied at once, and by the time the man reached the corner of Coloma Street a dozen loafers had caught up with him and started to put the rope about his neck. If it had not been for the prompt interference of Syd—who had proved his point as far as he cared to prove it, in a thoroughly scientific manner—the young man would have swung from the oak like Irish Dick.

When a criminal was due to be hanged, the sandhills of San Francisco "swarmed with human beings," wrote a disapproving Englishman. "They seemed clustered together like bees on a tree branch, and for the purpose of seeing a criminal convulsed and writhing in the agonies of a violent death! This desire seemed to pervade all classes of Americans in the city."

As sheriff and victim trudged through the streets, the bystanders rapidly snowballed behind them into a dense crowd. People in nearby houses leaned far out of second-story windows. In the clearing around the gibbet, the silent audience massed, quietly jockeying for best places while priest, sheriff and star performer played out the inexorable last act.

After a while the body hung limp, no longer kicking, swaying gently in the wind from the Bay. The show was over. Back to the city romped the mob in holiday mood, led by the Marion Rifles. When they reached the business district, the militia bands concluded the entertainment by going through a snappy drill on the Plaza.

Lively music and quick steppers in peacock uniforms—you can't deny Californians had a certain natural flair for executions. Truly the Argonaut bore little resemblance to his remote forbear, the austere and pious pioneer of Plymouth Rock. But this he and the Pilgrim had in common: both loved a duel, a dogfight, or a hanging day.

CHAPTER *13*

Sweet Betsey from Pike

Oh, do you remember Sweet Betsey from Pike
Who crossed the wide prairies with her lover, Ike,
With two yoke of oxen and one spotted hog,
A tall shanghai rooster, an old yaller dog?

Singing good-bye Pike County, good-bye for a while
We'll come back again when we've panned out our pile.
—Old Ballad

Parkhurst promised me some fine sport as he had nine
Pike Co. girls engaged.
—Franklin Buck.

Do you remember sweet betsey from pike?

You can't remember her because you never saw her. the best you can do is piece her together from old scraps of calico, like the endless intricate quilt she stitched by the light of an oil lamp while her foot in its black ugly boot, laced high, kept the cradle rocking.

Calico was the stuff her best dress was made of; she made it into a party gown by draping her precious silk shawl around the shoulders. She didn't "wear calico to the square dance" because this was a quaint novelty, so *chic*, but because she had nothing else to wear and a square dance was the only kind of dancing party there was for her.

She didn't "try to get a good tan"; on the contrary, she wore a sunbonnet to protect her complexion from the prairie sun—but, in spite of that, her skin was weathered like her frontiersman husband's and just as innocent of paint and powder as his. She had no time for

140

highfalutin styles of hairdress; she drew her hair skin tight back out of the way and fastened it so it would be the least possible bother.

She was a good woman, and she worked like a mule. She was the wife of the true pioneer—the man who had for generations driven into the sun with the aim of finding himself a bit of wilderness where he could build his own farm and live in complete independence. He was a stubborn man, a hard-living, hard-driving man who had pity neither for himself, his oxen, nor his woman, and who wanted above all to keep himself to himself and be beholden to nobody. When he happened to be going West during the gold-rush period, he pushed farther than he meant—or detoured from the Oregon Trail he typically followed—to discover what the big fuss was all about. For he was also a very inquisitive man. He and Betsey didn't necessarily come from Missouri or from Indiana, although they were tagged with the labels "Pike County" and "Hoosier." All settlers who were of typical middle western pioneer stock—usually poorly educated and dressed in rough homespun style—were called Hoosiers or Pike County people. They rode their prairie schooners out of many other spots along the westernmost fringe of the frontier, or from frontierlike areas further east, little islands of backwoods culture left behind as civilization spread west.

Betsey was tougher than her husband. Rescue parties who went into the mountains to save wagon trains ambushed by snow or starvation very often found the women were in better shape than the men. Sometimes the women had to take over the duties of the men—driving the oxen, foraging for food and wood—in addition to their own, when the men fell ill. The fierce strength, the unbeatable endurance of these women is almost unbelievable. They were as nearly unkillable as a human creature can get.

The Betseys and the upper-class señoritas from the ranchos were

141

few in number and as different from each other as raw whiskey is from honey, but they had some things in common. They were almost the only women already in California when the tidal wave of the gold rush broke upon the Bay. And both were an entirely different breed from the lady pirates who sailed in the wake of that wave. The rancho señoritas claimed aristocratic heritage and a portion of Spanish blood; they were carefully guarded, kept in luxury like beautiful parakeets in rich cages—shown off to, and barred off from, the Argonauts. For them, the world of the fandango-house señorita didn't exist. They were virtuous and so was Betsey, and there all resemblance ceased.

Pike County belles were conspicuous at all the first dances: "Their unique dress, combining the fashions of their foremothers with those which possibly may obtain among the fashionables of Australia, hang as gracefully on their flyaway figures, as they do themselves on the arms of their chevaliers." (All contemporary references to Australia are derogatory, because the continent at that time was one large-scale Devil's Island.)

Over and over again comes the disparaging commentary. The forty-niners respected Betsey for her sterling qualities, they paid homage to her as the only chaste woman they were likely to meet, they bought the pies she baked and crowded any boardinghouse she kept— but they didn't think she was pretty. Manlike, they worked her as they did their pack mules and then were disappointed if she didn't have the manners and the vivacious charm of a party girl.

Our Sonora observer, William Perkins, was interested in nothing so much as the different women who came his way. In 1851, after being exposed for two years to the French monte-dealing witches whose icy fascination he deplored, and the easy-living señoritas he liked but did not respect, Perkins recorded the fact that Sonora finally had the honor to welcome a "good woman":

142

Eureka! we all exclaimed a day or two ago, on the arrival of the wife and family of our American Doctor. But, good Lord! and I confess my very pen is blushing while it writes the sentence; the comparison is anything but favorable to morality. What chance has virtue in the shape of tall gawky, sallow, ill-dressed down easters, in rivalship with elegantly adorned, beautiful and graceful Vice! The strife is unequal. Virtue must put on some pleasing aspect to enable her to conquer the formidable enemy already entrenched so advantageously.

It is too much to expect from weak male human nature in California, that a man ever so correctly inclined, should prefer the lean arm of a bonnetted, ugly, board-shaped specimen of a descendant of the puritans, to the rosy cheeked, full formed, sprightly and elegant Spaniard or Frenchwoman, even with the full knowledge that the austerity of Virtue accompanies the one, while the dangerous fascination of Vice is hid under the exterior of the other.

But this was only one pioneer wife, sketched by one diarist—and a man who, we know by now, was not always trustworthy in his opinions of women because he was not objective about them. What did the other boys have to say about Betsey?

One gives patronizing approval to his dancing partners: "Some of them were rotten, on the backwoods order, but I found a much better sample of ladies than I expected to up here." The same writer mentions a hotelkeeper's promising him "fine sport as he had nine Pike Co. girls engaged," as if Betsey were a performing bear or something. Another contemporary illustrated her manners with an anecdote:

At a ball, given by the British Consul to celebrate the Queen's birthday, H—p—n asked a young lady to dance the next polka with him; she replied—
"No, sirra, I never promise a-head; first come, first served, is my ticket."

As if it were not bad enough to lambaste her manners and her costume, critics even questioned her fitness in her prize role, her job as a mother:

> What do you think of a lady taking a child 4 weeks old to a ball and having her husband hold it while she takes a trot with some of the hosts? There had to be a room appropriated for some of the mothers to nurse their children in.

If the forty-niners were disappointed in Betsey, very often they were also a bad influence upon her. Mrs. Sarah Royce (mother of Harvard philosopher Josiah Royce) described the effect of California on the only woman in Weaverville besides herself. This woman was about thirty-five. She was a plain person from a Western state, accustomed to country life. Very soon a boardinghouse keeper offered her a hundred dollars a month to cook three meals a day for his boarders (no dishwashing, and a cook's helper as an extra inducement). The next time Mrs. Royce saw her, she had dressed her hair up in a youthful fashion and decked herself out in a fancy new gown with full trimmings; she was "shining in society," and generously wanting to share her luck, asked Mrs. Royce to come with her to a dance at Hangtown. "It gave me a glimpse," wrote Mrs. Royce, "of the ease with which the homeliest if not the oldest, might become a 'belle' in those early days. . . ." Apparently the nouveau-riche effect of Betsey in borrowed peacock plumes was slightly appalling.

Poor Betsey! Today they put up statues to her, but in those days they made a joke of her. Naturally she wanted a good time. Naturally, being female, she was in demand in spite of what the boys said behind her back. She came to the gold-town dance with high expectations. She stood in the doorway with her lanky six-foot husband and glanced about with quick bold curiosity, noting every detail of the one-room bachelor's hotel converted into a ballroom for the night: on one side the counter and goods of a store, on the opposite side rows of bunks for the lodgers camouflaged bashfully with draperies of red calico. And she prepared to enjoy herself after her own fashion.

> On ball-nights the bar was closed, and everything was very quiet and respectable. To be sure, there was some danger of being swept away in a flood of tobacco-juice, but luckily the floor was uneven, and it lay around in puddles, which with care one could avoid, merely running the minor risk of falling prostrate upon the wet boards in the midst of a gallopade.
> Of course the company was made up principally of the immigrants. Such dancing, such dressing, and such conversation, surely was never heard or seen before. The gentlemen were compelled to have a regular fight with their fair partners before they could drag them onto the floor. I am happy to say that almost always the stronger vessel won the day . . . except in the case of certain timid youths who, after one or two attacks, gave up the battle in despair.

The cultivated lady who attended and described this ball night (the famous belletrist, Dame Shirley) had a lower opinion of Betsey than even the ungrateful Argonaut.

Whatever he might say about Betsey, the forty-niner was not above fighting over her. When the landlord of Selby Flat's hotel gave a party, "All the women were there—seven of them—and about two hundred men. They had a fiddler—Mart Simonson; one of the best I ever heard. It was great sport for a while, but towards morning some of the men got too much gin aboard and a quarrel started about the right to dance with one of the Missouri girls. Pistols were drawn, the lights put out, at least a hundred shots fired; but, funny enough,

145

only one man was hurt—Sam Creeley, who was hit in the leg. I went out through a window and did not wait to see the finish. It was too exciting for me."

This proportion of women to men was about average for back-country dances. At Nevada City's first ball early in 1850 there were twelve ladies to three hundred men. The men wore red or blue flannel shirts tucked into their high boots, and clanked through the rollicking hoedown steps with bowie knife and revolver keeping an offbeat rhythm. The ladies came from all over the country, in clean bright cotton dresses and plaid silk or wool shawls, and their best high calf boots. In order to compensate for the disproportion of the sexes, "A number of the men tied handkerchiefs around their arms and airily assumed the character of ballroom belles."

For all their love of dancing and their criticism of Betsey's ballroom manners, the gentlemen were not necessarily such skillful exemplars of the rhythmic art themselves. Franklin Buck tells it on himself:

> You may remember that I was overgrown and awkward but at the last ball, as I was dancing with the belle of the salon "Madame Chabord," I trod on her flounce and ripped her skirt about halfway round the waist, I overheard one fellow say to another: "Why Buck is much lighter than I imagined a man of his size to be. He handles himself very gracefully on the floor." So you see I have gotten over that failing of my youth.

Betsey had a lot to put up with, and she was the girl who could do it. Anything for a good time. Apparently she had the same iron endurance for pleasure as she had for work.

> Talk about our grandmothers, etc., in early times riding to parties and meetings—four ladies came over from Shasta, 40 miles, on mules, Saturday and Sunday. Monday they ran

all over town, calling. At night they danced, ate and drank till two o'clock. The next day the same and dancing all night. They started home at daylight and rode 40 miles over the worst mountains you ever did see.

Of course the kind of dancing party composed of one Betsey to every ten or twelve rough-but-decent miners was not the only kind of ball in California during the stag-party stage of the rush. There were other dances where every kind of headdress *but* sunbonnet was featured, the wild parties starring harlequin masque and *rebozo;* and there were also the stately balls at the ranchos, where the high-caste native Californians indolently lent their señoritas as dancing partners, but never took their eyes off their woman for an instant.

Best description of the early masquerade ball comes from the pen of Frank Soulé, a pen which he seemed to dip in brandy more often than ink. No contemporary writer was capable of deploring sin with such muscular enthusiasm as this young journalist. He notes the initial all-male society, and then tells us that very soon women joined the crowd and new pleasures appeared. "Then reason tottered and passion ran riot. The allurements of the cyprian contested the scepter with the faro banks." ("Cyprian" was a favorite contemporary euphemism for prostitute.) The combination of riotous passion and Cyprians led of course in one direction, and reason tottered rapidly off to the great hall where the masquerade ball was going on.

This hall—the California Exchange—was about a hundred feet square, with a fifty-foot bar covered with gold leaf and decorated with hundreds of bottles and decanters, topped off with a golden eagle perched over the liquor supply. "The American cannot drink a cocktail comfortably unless the 'star-spangled banner' float above, and the national eagle look with at least a glassy eye into his potations; in the center a piece of machinery, exhibiting the sea in motion, tossing

147

a laboring ship upon its bosom; a water-mill in action; a train of cars passing over a bridge," and other such childish mechanical toys. Opposite, of course, a full band, and on the third side—chaste note!— a coffee-and-cake stand.

About nine o'clock the guests began to arrive, paid their money to the ticket taker, allowed the policeman to frisk them for weapons (no clanking of knives and guns allowed at these parties) and deposited umbrellas. The currently popular masquer types included Spanish bandits, Gypsies, Bloomer girls (a good one, she was "beautiful in short skirts and satin-covered extremities" in an age when the glimpse of a lady's ankle was supposed to be thrilling), French counts, Turks, Poles, and Swiss ballad singers. (Also present was the "curious, but respectable lady, hidden by cloak and false visage," which if true adds a provocative footnote. What was she doing there if she was so chaste?)

These strange apparitions at once chose partners and went crashing away through the gallopade, the waltz, the mazurka, interrupting their violent exertions with trips to the bar or the coffeestand. Towards morning the liquor was operating on everyone, fights started up, and "woman, forgetting her last prerogative, gentleness, joins the ring and gives point and effect to feminine oaths, by the use of feminine nails." What the ladies had to fight about, when there was such a superfluity of men, is hard to discover; but many a masquerade ended with broken furniture, smashed bottles, and hair-pulling contests. As dawn approached, the milder spirits began prudently withdrawing from the field, "the first departing being careful to select the finest umbrellas," and the masquerade sagged to a bleary finish in a haze of bruised shins, drunken lovers and torn dominos. Tickets for a big brawl like this cost five dollars; an ordinary run-of-the-mill fandango hall charged only three, but you could get in for nothing if you brought

148

a woman with you—and were prepared to be generous with her.

This kind of party, of course, was not inhibited by the stuffy respectability of Betsey or the watchfulness of the jealous dons. If you were lucky and met the right people, you might get an invitation to a high-class ranchero party. While Betsey was rather a milk-porridge creature socially (wholesome but unexciting), the señorita was something else again: exotic, coquettish, dressed in a gay and seductive simplification of an old civilization's sophisticated fashion. Furthermore, decorous and duennaed as she was, she seemed to be as fascinated with the tall, blond, blue-eyed gringo as he was with her.

Señoritas were in such demand that when a ball was scheduled, men came around weeks beforehand clamoring for the privilege of escorting them, and always sent carriages after them. No black-eyed ranchero's daughter went to an American ball on foot. Nothing was too much if it would please her. Did she insist upon a japonica blossom for her hair? Her suitor hurried to the best florist shop he knew. There he found a circle of men staring anxiously at one lone japonica, the last in town.

"How much?" inquired the cavalier.

"Forty dollars."

"I'll take it," said our hero, counting out his nuggets.

The señoritas came to the dance in white muslin dresses with tiny waists and skirts ankle length to give provocative glimpses of slim silken legs. (When Betsey shared honors with her at a ball, Betsey noted with jealous scorn that the flouncing hemlines also revealed an occasional flash of yellow or scarlet wool petticoat.) The men were dressed in "sky-blue velvet pants, open at the sides and rows of buttons, with white drawers, red sash and a fancy shirt." Men and women alike were smoking "cigaritos." The starched white skirts of the Spanish girls "stretched so stiffly that you could not get very near," but they were lovely to look at. If the señorita felt especially elated by the look in blue Yankee eyes, sometimes she dared that look with a solo dance, "making more noise with her little feet and slippers than I could with thick boots," wrote an admirer. He added enthusiastically, "Their cotillions are the same as ours except that the last figure is 'all promenade to the Bar,' where you and your fair partner imbibe." This last figure became a normal part of all California cotillions, since the Yankees seemed to regard it as an excellent improvement on the style of home.

Customs of the native fandango were exotic enough to hold the strongest possible appeal for the forty-niners. There were, however, occasions when civilizations clashed on the ballroom floor, and the oil-and-water mixture of Betsey and señorita ruined the party.

Sonora's grand Christmas ball suffered this fate. There were too many Yankees in town who looked down on "those greasy foreigners" who had settled and established the town. The ball began, according to native California custom, at two o'clock in the afternoon. But instead of lasting the customary two days and two nights without intermission, it dwindled to a sullen halt shortly after midnight that same day!

Why did this ball last only a paltry twelve hours? Why did the disgruntled dons vote it "a perfect humbug, an arrant cheat and take in . . . less pork for a shilling" than their three pesos ever bought before? (Surely a free Pike translation of California Spanish!)

They held this unfavorable opinion because some of "the Hoosier *elite* voted waltzing a perfect bore, and decidedly an uninteresting and vulgar dance, as well as the *hota* and other Castilian figures . . . and would have none of it. 'Ole Kanetuck,' and Missouri, and Oregon 'hoe-downs,' were the only elegant and graceful performances of the kind permitted." The dons should have brought their own dance band

150

and let the Spanish guitarists and the square-dance fiddlers cut each other.

At Marysville's first successful ball, it was impossible to scare up either Betseys or señoritas in any reasonable number. The ladies discovered they were only seven. Before the party began, they persuaded a minister's son from Boston to dress in hoops and crinoline. With much giggling they assembled a wardrobe for him, each one contributing what she could spare, here a fan and there a shawl and from some wealthy female even a handsome gown.

When they heard the fiddler strike up "The Arkansas Traveler," they shepherded their protégé into the hall and solemnly introduced him as a visiting sister from the East.

The men were charmed. The Boston boy blushed and simpered and fiddled with his fan. Miners crowded around him, vying for the honor of dancing with him. He was the belle of the ball that evening— and half the night was gone before any of his partners discovered he was no lady.

What better comment could you want on the high degree of respectability Betsey was introducing into gold-rush society? She was coming into town, she and her aristocratic cousin from New England who waited until California looked safe and then sailed round the Horn. They were moving in, first slowly, later more rapidly, carrying Virtue like a banner above their strong-minded, sensible, sunbonneted heads. And for better or worse, they were changing the moral climate.

PART TWO

The Morning After

CHAPTER *14*

Dawn of the Morning After

CAN ANYBODY NOTE THE EXACT MOMENT WHEN THE MIRAGE OF EL DORADO BEGAN TO FADE AND THE MORE PROSAIC REALITY OF A SOUND agricultural state began to take its place? That's like trying to draw a pencil line between dawn and the workaday sunshine of full morning.

After all, the mirage on the edge of the Pacific is not completely faded yet. Instead of mining camps electrified with the frantic excitement of the Big Strike, we have the golden alleys of Hollywood. Instead of bonanza glamour, we have the dream of spending one's declining years in an atmosphere officially dedicated to a Garden-of-Eden climate.

No one could say dogmatically that *any* year marked the end of a westward drift of the dreamers, the unstable, the restless ones, the glamour hunters.

Yet certain sobering changes were under way from the first. Unheard beneath the roaring full-throated orchestration of the bonanza symphony was the steady, sure motif of sensible commercial consolidation and progress. As early as 1852 hydraulic mining was making its first inroads upon the individualistic panning and pickax methods of the independent prospector. By the middle of the decade, organized companies furnished with the latest quartz-mining equipment were

155

stolidly raping the Sierra, and the day of the free-lance treasure hunter was closing in California.

As this happened the froth of the forty-niners, the professional prospectors and congenital wanderers, began trailing away after a less exploited pot of gold and the diggings became less romance and more Big Business. Some, of course, stayed in the camps to become the "old-timers" of legend. Many amateur miners, who had come to "see the elephant" and enjoy a year's wild-oat cultivation, returned East to their regular homes and jobs. Some of them found the East stifling after their free years and came back to California with their families to settle down to restaurantkeeping, exporting, professional services and other normal ways of making a living. Many took what capital they had managed to save from the harpies of the gambling hells and invested it in grocery stores or hotels. Successful miners looked around them and saw what the Pike County folks had seen from the beginning: that this was a wonderful place for a farm. Unsuccessful ones, tired of the search and ashamed to go home empty-handed, found jobs on the docks of San Francisco or in the numerous building projects. By the end of the decade, the great wheat ranches were already beginning to stretch themselves in the hot sun, rippling with a paler gold that would soon outshine the great bonanza itself.

San Francisco, repeatedly built and rebuilt upon the ashes of its burned-over shacks, began settling into a solid and well-constructed city of stone and brick. Gone were Happy Valley, the stick-and-newspaper huts, the canvas magic-lantern village. In its place, like the classic barmaid-into-princess transformation of the fairy tale, arose a bold and sturdy hoyden city with an increasingly convincing make-up job, designed to impress beholders with her culture and Victorian respectability.

This settling process resulted partly from a steady shift in dominant population types as adventurers moved on toward new gold discoveries; as the less adventurous turned from the elephant to the plow horse and yoke of oxen; as "men of substance," sensing the real commercial potential of the frontier state, arrived with their families by every ship. The process was also influenced by other economic factors allied with the precarious status of gold itself. The dangerously inflated gold-rush economy was beginning to feel warning twinges of deflation before 1853, and by 1855 it tottered like a baby's block tower, ready to crash if the faintest breeze blew on it.

The breeze that blew in from the East was more like a high wind: in St. Louis the suspension of the parent house of San Francisco's leading bankers, Page and Beacon, touched off a run on the California house which in turn struck ruin to powerful Adams and Company. The Adams Banking and Express Company stretched like a great vine across the state; no town or camp was too small for an Adams branch to have a grip there. When Adams crashed, it pulled innumerable individuals and separate businesses to earth along with it, and California suffered its first siege of business panic and depression.

It was high time California discovered a firmer foundation for its quivering economy than the golden quicksands of the Big Rock Candy Mountain.

Certain reigning delights of a gold rush culture fitted a dazed and jolted depression population no better than a fat rich uncle's overcoat fits his scrawny poor-relation nephew. It is much easier to be well behaved when you have no money for monte or whiskey.

Along with economic changes came the steady sure invasion of westering wives. Respectable women took a look around the golden state and went busily to work straightening up its moral bureau drawers. But they were not always immune to the provocation of the

157

stray japonica, the crumpled bit of lace, that they found in those bureau drawers; and they were not always above trying on in secret this or that tawdry luscious souvenir the scorned predecessor had left behind when she was evicted.

By and large, the Argonaut was glad to see his proper Victorians. Every schoolboy knows vacation palls in time, and license to raise hell —if it comes too easily and lasts too long—can lose its charm.

The big spree had been roaring good fun, but now the socks were gone completely to holes and the shirts worn out, and it was good to see Mama—even Mama with her rules and regulations, her corseted and crinolined social system, her genteel tea-drinkings and her horror of bawdy indecencies and rowdy pleasures: after all, she was the girl who brought the aspirin.

And the hangover was getting pretty bad.

CHAPTER *15*

Ice Cream Saloons

THERE WERE CITIZENS OF EL DORADO WHO WOULD HAVE LAUGHED BIT-
TERLY IF YOU HAD PRAISED THE GAIETY AND EXCITEMENT OF GOLD
rush days. Maybe it was supposed to be an exciting place, but the
Alverson girls, who had to live in it, found it unbearably dull. No
young lady ever complained more furiously of the tedium of Main
Street than they complained of Stockton. It was no capital, like
Sacramento or San Jose, nor center of citified pleasures like San
Francisco. It was nothing but a dingy way station on the road to
the southern mines.

True enough, Stockton had amusements of a sort. There was a
gambling house right across the street and a saloon halfway down the
block, to mention only those in one's immediate neighborhood. But
eventually you got bored with peeking from behind the drapes to see
if any of father's friends went into the fandango house. Most of the
time there was just no fun for a proper girl in Stockton.

On Christmas, 1852, Stockton changed overnight for the Alver-
sons. When the oldest sister came downstairs that morning, she walked
into the parlor and there was her present: a piano. No Eastern girl
could understand what that piano meant to her and her sisters. It was
the only piano in Stockton.

Christmas night, after the curtains were drawn and the candles lit,
Miss Alverson brought sheet music out of the wooden chest where she
had hoarded it, and placed it on the rack. There in the candlelight, with

friends and gifts and the crisp evergreen scent all around her, she hesitantly began picking out the tunes her fingers half remembered— "Annie Laurie," "Coming Through the Rye," "Ben Bolt," all the sweet and innocent old ballads of home. One by one voices joined in and followed the tremulous thread of melody a girl played on her new piano.

> It was like a new world, such unexpected happiness . . . [wrote her sister]. Father had occasion to answer a call at the front door and before closing it he accidentally looked out, and to his surprise the sidewalks and porch were filled with old and young men. Along the side of the house stood scores of men in the street as far as the eye could see, and some were sobbing.

Mr. Alverson drew back the curtains as far as they would go, and the homeless men outside the windows joined in the ballads and Christmas carols the girls were singing on the candlelit side of the windows. To them, as to the sisters, it was a piece of the old life torn out and magically set down in the midst of the new.

The fandango house across the street had real competition that Christmas.

As pure young ladies with pianos grew more numerous, many a forty-niner was lured out of the gambling hells to the dignified family parlor where (after carefully depositing his revolver in the hall) he might lean on the instrument and watch the earnest face of his accompanist as he lent an obedient baritone to "When the Swallows Homeward Fly." If he had a guitar or a fiddle, the young lady would be delighted to have him bring it along. It was easy to pick up the tune of "Cant d'Amour," "Do I Not Love Thee?", "The Magyar Polka," and the like. Certainly it was worth trying, for the sake of the soulful admiration his efforts aroused in the blue eyes of the pianist.

160

For people whose intellectual tastes put them above such trifles, it was possible to buy music-hawkers' arrangements of arias from "Rigoletto," and "Il Trovatore," or a fine setting of "With Verdure Clad" from the oratorio *Creation*. And hymns were always popular and suitable.

If this was the day of shooting affrays and saloon society, it was also the period of the language of flowers, the etiquette of the fan, and songs advertised in all seriousness as: "A beautiful thing, and would be very destructive if well sung, to the gentleman who turned the leaves for the lady; so much could be implied, and yet the lady remain perfectly non-committal." Such was Cupid's double-talk in the 1850's: a dangerously destructive ballad, loaded with implications.

The more young ladies in California, the less employment of Colt's revolvers and the wider reliance on lethal weapons like that one.

Carrying on diplomatic relations with young ladies led the forty-niner along paths not at all consistent with the popular portrait of him as a crude hairy brute. There was the lady's sweet tooth to consider—and while he was at it, he might as well consider his own. Sweet shops began springing up between the saloons like wild violets claiming a bit of earth in a rank poppy bed. An English candyman in a tall black narrow-rimmed hat trundled his pushcart about the San Francisco streets, crying "Hore-hound, Peppermint and Wintergreen! Large lumps! and strongly flavored! 'Ere they *go!*" And then in his drill-sergeant voice he would shout the names of prominent customers, judges and colonels, and sometimes even the names of ladies these gentlemen courted with his candies. This procedure was dangerous, however; if the customer overheard he was likely to take offense upon hearing his lady's name bandied about the streets and threaten violent action.

First of the sweetsellers was Jerry Regan, who stirred his candy kettle in Happy Valley in the earliest days of San Francisco and hawked fresh peppermint and horehound around the canvas city for a quarter a stick. He did very well for himself, since all other candy came around the Horn without benefit of cellophane.

But the most successful, the real Horatio Alger boy of the candy and soft drink business, was that wild revolutionary character, M. L. Winn.

When Winn came to California in 1849, he was nothing but a candymonger, making candies in his little steam factory and hawking them personally around the muddy streets of San Francisco. But he was a very peculiar pioneer, a mixture of equal parts shrewd business sense and radical notions. His radical notions were two: in wet, wild California, he believed a refreshment house could make money without selling anything alcoholic; in womanless California, he believed it was smarter to appeal to women than to men. He was all in favor of women in a day when the mere phrases "bloomer girl" or "women's rights" called for a laugh. The thing he most believed in about women was their queenly power over the money of men.

Obviously, the man was crazy; obviously he was heading for bankruptcy. But he never got there. He took his two funny ideas and his sharp Yankee nose for trading and built the first California soda fountain into Big Business.

Winn was betting on the fact that ladies didn't drink in public, and that ladies would be coming to California. Respectable women might sip a little wine in the privacy of their home, but a man couldn't take a lady into a saloon for the evening if it turned out that he knew a lady and needed a place to take her. When there began to be ladies he could take out, the forty-niner began looking around to see if there was any spot where he and a proper Victorian could dawdle over the lady's kind of drink: liquids like ginger pop, lemon syrup, root beer, "sarsaparilla beer."

In the back country he was out of luck for a while—but in the back country there were few ladies to take anywhere. In San Francisco, Winn was ready for him. There the forty-niner knew where to go when the company he kept forced him into spending a sober evening. If he hadn't heard, he could find out by a quick glance at the papers:

BY MOONLIGHT.—Lovers with their sweethearts, and husband with their better-halves go promenading these charming moonlight nights, in every direction, yet one point "WINN'S FOUNTAIN HEAD" seems to attract the attention of all, for visit there when you will, a crowd of the fairest of the fair, with their natural protectors, whom someone has styled the lords of creation, may be seen regaling themselves with ice creams, strawberries and cream, oysters in every style, and other choice dishes too numerous to mention.

N.B. No private rooms or boxes are attached to these Saloons, as no one visits here who is not willing to see and be seen.

Providing you were willing to see and be seen—that is providing the fair one you were naturally protecting wasn't troubled with legal ties to some jealous man—you couldn't find a better spot than Winn's principal "refectory" or the branch which his skyrocketing popularity forced him to build to take care of the overflow.

Winn began by taking the profits from his candy push wagon and investing them in the "STEAM CANDY MANUFACTORY AND FANCY PIE AND CAKE BAKERY." The factory had an annex—a little room added on almost as an afterthought, with a counter in it and a couple of benches. But this modest cubbyhole contained a seed like the bean that Jack planted. Before Winn knew it he was almost as busy with his building as his cooking. He expanded the tiny room into a good-sized hall; this still wasn't enough, so he set up the branch out on Washington and Montgomery. By 1854 his combined ice cream saloons seated four hundred and fifty people at a time; he took care of three thousand customers a day on an average, and his record sale for ice cream alone was fifteen hundred servings in a day.

Pretty good, for a crazy Yankee full of radical notions about temperance and woman's rights.

Mary Jane Megquier tells us the place "surpasses any thing I have seen in the states, very large windows with magnificent buff silk damask curtains with lace like those that Newhall Sturtevant boasts so much of, two large rooms are connected by an arch hung with the same material, marble tables, floors and counters and as light as day at all hours of the night, the homeliest man in the city treated me to an ice cream there a few nights since at one dollar a glass."

Mary Jane was a decent respectable wife from New England who wouldn't be seen in a saloon. But the "homeliest man in the city" was *not* Mary Jane's husband. One of the things Mary Jane liked about California comes out in an earlier letter home: ". . . there is no scandal every one is his own man, not a word about such a thing is not respectable, you know I always detested that . . ." California—with its air of freedom and its ice cream saloons where you could drop in for an evening with gentleman friends and not arouse a lot of silly gossip—suited Mary Jane and a good many other respectable but convention-hating females very well indeed.

People came to laugh at M. L. Winn and his ice cream saloons; they lingered to watch with astonishment, and they stayed to imitate. Thanks to him and those who copied him, there were "fountains" in the fifties as today where wives out shopping could drop in for lunch, high school boys and girls pause for refreshment on the way home from school, or young men escort their ladies when weary of standing in the parlor turning the pages of devastating ballads.

164

CHAPTER *16*

Playgrounds and Sulphur Springs

IN THE STAG-PARTY CULTURE OF EL DORADO, THE SALOON WAS EVERY-MAN'S CLUB, THE GAMBLING HELL HIS HEARTH FIRE, THE FANDANGO cellar and the bullfight arena his playground. If this didn't suit him, he could stay home.

Families don't play like that. The families that came pouring into San Francisco in the fifties wanted something else, and they got it. If they were aristocratic families, they scorned the resulting institutions as "common." But if they were middle-class, easy-going, pleasure-seeking people (especially if they were German), they had just what they wanted.

In 1849 the plank road to the Mission Dolores led a roistering male clientele out to the bullfight. By the mid-fifties it led a carriage procession of sportive picnickers to Russ's Garden.

Across the sand dunes where the forty-niners once cheered for the bull, Henry Russ laid out the sprawling walks, restaurants, pavilions and playfields of San Francisco's first and favorite playground.

Swings hung from the oaks of Russ's Garden. Arbors, green-houses and summerhouses offered shelter to lovers while they strolled to the tunes of the "promenade concert." Mama spread the tablecloth and the picnic out on the lawn, and, on the other side of the flower-bordered walks, the head of the house found his bowling alleys and billiard tables, and the young athlete strove with bar, ring and weights to demonstrate his muscles to the admiring young lady.

"Here beer foamed, waltzers whirled, balloons ascended." Here every Sunday morning the sun streamed through the high windows of the Mammoth Pavilion upon the flushed faces of the dancers, crinoline and sporty suit swirling like leaves in a whirlwind through the dizzy intricacies of that vulgar innovation, the waltz. Russ's Garden had two orchestras, innumerable flower beds, classic (but modest) plaster statues, and the right kind of space and equipment for cricket matches, baseball games, races and other clean sports. It was as decent, strenuous, and plebeian as the rosy-faced well-scrubbed German youngsters from the *Turnverein* who waltzed there.

Farther out along the Mission Road was another playground, the Willows. It was more remote, but this in itself was an advantage to picnickers who wanted to make a day of it, and the place offered the big attraction of a zoo full of bears and sea lions. Sea lions were a particular curiosity to newcomers and impressed some travelers as one of the most amusing phenomena in the new state. The Willows advertised its "romantic setting": through the center of the garden trickled a winding creek, fringed with water grasses and the drooping trees that gave the place its name. In 1861 the creek flooded and washed out the entire garden.

The public gardens that sprang up in all the cities during the late fifties and early sixties were never popular with the newly rich bluebloods of the state. Nevertheless, for the incoming mass of middleclass citizens—neither tycoons nor brawling Argonauts—they were what the city parks and seaside boardwalks are to pleasure hunters today.

Another recreation of the later fifties, as typically Victorian as the gambling hell was typically gold rush, was the excursion. It was the

166

more elaborate and expensive version of a picnic trip to the gardens. Steamboat excursions—"water frolics"—were organized and advertised in glowing terms by promoters whose keen rivalry forced them to provide all kinds of inducements on shipboard—bands playing, dancing on the deck, rich refreshments. While the boat ride itself was supposed to be the main part of the party, the excursion usually had a specific destination: Mare Island, the Farallon Islands, or various picnic spots along the Carquinez Straits. Sometimes they were fishing expeditions. A "chowder party" would chug out around Mare Island in pursuit of shellfish. Everybody brought a small rowboat in which to shove off from the mother ship and go poking around among the mussel-bearing rocks.

But excursions, like all other social events in California life, were more an occasion for drinking and dancing than for fishing or going places. The place you might get to or the shellfish you might collect were incidental to the general air of revelry. Given this atmosphere, the excursion of the Dashaway Society in 1859 sounded a loud bugle call of changing customs.

Breaking sharply with California tradition, the Dashaways organized an excursion on a basis that would have astonished the man of 'forty-nine as much as the sudden appearance of a side-wheeler on the brook-sized upper reaches of the Mokelumne River. They served no liquor.

The Dashaway Society, already becoming a power in San Francisco, was a temperance union dedicated to the truism that you could catch more flies with honey than you could with vinegar. Instead of screaming about the evils of Demon Rum, they planned nonalcoholic parties to show people what fun they could have without a drink. On this particular steamer day, they crowded twelve hundred strong onto the *San Antonio* and set off amid cheers and loud *William Tell* band music for Mare Island. At noon they pulled up alongside the U.S. frigate *Independence* and, on the decks of a ship hoary with history even then, they devoured their cold chicken, sipped their ginger beer, and danced quadrilles—thus proving to their own satisfaction that fun didn't have to come in a bottle.

Nonalcoholic excursions were, however, confined to the social outings of temperance societies.

Sometimes steamer trips proved far more exciting than anyone expected. The captains, anxious to race their ships faster than rival ships, goaded the engines beyond their capacity. As a result, much too often the steamships blew up. This possibility was an added thrill.

In a state so recently a sleepy Mexican colony and a wild frontier, one would not expect the "escape from the city" idea to be a very important motive in amusement seeking. Yet Californians no sooner had their centers of urban civilization than they began planning their vacations in the country. While the mining-camp people still trekked downstream to San Francisco to see the wild ladies, the urban dwellers were packing their camp kits and journeying into the interior to see the wild flowers.

Country vacations came in at least two flavors. For the less energetic, there were summer resorts and "spas." People who wanted something more adventurous could travel farther to gaze upon some of the scenic marvels that press agents already publicized.

California summer resorts boasted wildly about the magic properties of their mineral waters, and as a result they were appropriately haunted by the descendants of Ponce de Leon. They were also extremely fashionable—and in that day, as in this, social custom required that fashionable females wear the right kind of furs and jewels and vacation at the proper places. Above all summer resorts were licensed game reserves for fortune hunters and overflowed every season with simpering young ladies going through their paces under the steely eyes of ambitious mothers. The completely parasitic lady of fashion was as typical of the fifties as the overworked sunbonnet women of the pioneer home—though naturally more rare, as the considerable income required to support this human bird of paradise limited her numbers.

The mineral springs at Sonoma provided the site of one of the first California resorts to bid for the patronage of the carriage trade, as well as the lame and the halt. Right in the middle of a highly advertised climate, its promoters built a house directly over one of the springs. The house contained ten bathing rooms, private cubbyholes where a person could loll in the tepid water of the "salubrious" sulphur springs as long as he could stand the odor. The fact that it smelled like that was solid proof that it had to be good for you.

In the long, low, white-painted hotels, hemmed with porches and piazzas where hammocks tempted to indolence, city dwellers slept a country sleep and revived their stale appetites with country food. The need to do this proved how civilized they were. The popular White Sulphur Springs near Napa was set in a thickly wooded canyon beside a creek where pale ferns and yellow monkey flowers leaned over the water and rustic bridges crisscrossed at intervals. Along the stream clustered the white springhouses, "arbors built over the springs and covered with vines." Up over the mountainside, shady trails wound in and out around crags and boulders, leading the more energetic up to a peak where they looked upon the valley spread out below like a green fan.

During the evenings, guests danced in the rustic ballroom, or drove across wagon roads to Calistoga Hot Springs where a smaller whitewashed inn "accommodated a few guests," wrote a socialite, and "accommodated also a rattlesnake the day we lunched there." Rattlesnakes and tarantulas were among the hazards that assured the urban visitor he was getting the real basic country living.

As in an earlier day the forty-niner would travel long distances to see a female, later in the fifties parties of city women journeyed into the gold country to get a look at a bona fide prospector. These pleasure parties basked self-consciously in the glamour of gold, rhapsodized over the picturesque miner planted hip-deep in the stream, patiently washing the golden sand through his sieve, and gathered twittering at the river brink, playfully begging for a turn at the panning.

Occasionally one of these ladies came across a strike in a region others believed to be washed up. When this occurred, seasoned natives winked at each other behind the ecstatic gold hunter's back, knowing that some practical joker had salted the ground. Today, with nuggets far rarer than they could have seemed even to these naive urbanites, one can't help thinking the joke was on the humorist who played such expensive tricks on greenhorns.

Here was progress: in '49 gold was everybody's business; by '60 there was a sharp line between mountain dwellers to whom prospecting was still a way of life and newcomers capable of taking a tourist's eye view of the diggings and an "isn't it quaint?" attitude toward all that had been most backbreakingly vital to the forty-niner.

Unspoiled little mining villages were not the only attraction that drew vacationers into the Sierra Nevadas. Smart businessmen had already discovered the possibilities of one of California's biggest businesses: the Wonder Business. One of the first Wonders to be commercially exploited was the *Sequoia gigantea,* largest and oldest of living things.

James Sperry started the exploitation of the red giants with a modest hotel in Murphy's Camp, a mining town in Calaveras County of jumping-frog fame. Customers still had to pack twenty miles to see the Mammoth Grove. Enough of them did this to convince Sperry it was wise to build a hotel in the grove itself. Thousands of city-dwelling sight-seers came to this crude lodge to look up at the tall trees. Guidebooks and newspaper advertisements gave names to individual sequoias, such as Father of the Forest, Bride of the Forest, and so forth. Most of the bark was stripped from the Mother of the Forest, much of it sent to the exhibition at the Crystal Palace in London, and the Mother died of it and crashed to earth in the next big storm. Souvenir hunters, then as now, were not above taking a bit of bark to show the people back home.

Commercialization of the tourist appeal of the Sierras—not yet under any control by government agencies—was well under way. Eighteen fifty-nine saw the opening of a resort hotel many miles beyond Sperry's redwood lodge. This new establishment was located in a deep narrow gorge in the heart of the Sierra Nevada, which had been discovered by a white man turned Indian chief, the notorious Jim Savage. It was almost inaccessible, but it offered a miraculous spectacle of slender misty waterfalls chalking white perpendiculars around the canyon walls. When spring thaws opened the snowbound trails, it could be reached by an arduous two-day pack trip in from Coulterville.

It seemed highly unlikely that any hotel such a long hard journey away from civilization could ever draw enough customers to stay in business. There must have been many who laughed about the supreme folly of trying to set up a summer resort way off there in the Yosemite Valley.

CHAPTER *17*

Horse Opera: Mammoth Version

As EL DORADO SETTLED AND SOLIDIFIED INTO THE STATE OF CALIFORNIA, ITS CITIZENS—SETTLERS, HOMEOWNERS, NO LONGER PROSPECTORS ONLY —looked around for a pattern to fit their pride, and found it. Everything was bigger here; everything was "more so." And the word for it was "mammoth."

If you had to stay in town and miss the Mammoth Grove, there were plenty of other mammoth attractions all around. San Francisco show business in the later fifties, given the support of culture seekers and women customers, had won complete ascendancy over the earlier stag-party amusement center, the gambling hell. But theater, reflecting the society it served, resembled nothing so much as a rapidly twirling kaleidoscope of mammoth proportions.

Peering in, one catches a glimpse of a notorious courtesan, a bit of Verdi, magic and mesmerism, extravaganza, and horse opera with real opera and real horses, but no cowboys. What pattern does it make? Hardly any. Each glittering scrap slips out of sight or into a new formation before one can see it fairly, and the total impression is of brilliant chaos, wild excitement, a wealth of talent, and very little result in terms of theater art. Impresarios flashed into the spotlight, threw money around frantically, dazzled everyone with elaborate sets and costumes and rushed into bankruptcy with the same meteoric speed.

Competition was fierce. Circus, that pioneer of the entertainment world, fought bankruptcy with barnstorming tours and desperate elaboration of its acts.

Not only was Shakespeare performed in the pungent atmosphere of lions and horses, but circus acts themselves cashed in on the current rage for extravaganza. It was fashionable for equestrians to play would-be tragic roles on horseback. The Colonel himself was famous for his portrayal of the Emperor's Envoy, or the Russian Messenger. (If a role looked good under one title, it looked twice as good under two.) He performed this equestrian monologue on several horses at once, somewhat as follows:

> The envoy becomes nearly frozen; despair with iron rule possesses his almost sinking heart; when, nerving himself, and animating his sinking horses, he espies the steeple tops and minarets of gay St. Petersburg; and the brightness of inspiring hope renews the spring of his activity, he reaches home, embraces his only boy, presenting a fine and forcible picture of joy and gratitude.

Rowe wasn't the only one to go in for things like this. In his troupe he starred the versatile Miss Whittaker, who included in her repertoire an impersonation of an Indian Dancing Girl, Lucette the Village Coquette, and a *Sylphide of the Upper Air* in which she was a mythological immortal in love with a mere man. All these acts and others she performed while keeping her balance on the broad jogging back of her horse, displaying with exquisite co-ordination what one enthusiast termed "the unchecked joy of her bounding heart." Her final number brought the horse right into the act, as it was entitled *Zanthe Driven Mad by Her Own Infuriated Horse*. This should sur-

173

prise nobody, as any normal horse would be near the breaking point by that time.

But if the circus stole from melodrama, the theater reciprocated in kind. In the fifties horse opera was not a figure of speech meaning mere cowboys and Indians. It was high tragedy plus onstage horses. Most famous of these horse operas was *Mazeppa*, in which a horse co-starred with the heroine. All the nonsense of this play built up to an equestrienne tour de force: at the grand climax, the wild horse Mazeppa rescued the heroine, who was bound to his broad back while he galloped around the stage and up a steep hill, between perilous crags and so offstage. Traditionally a male played the heroine. At that, they often anticlimaxed the play by putting a dummy on Mazeppa for the dangerous ride.

Adah Isaacs Menken changed all that. In the early sixties, she treated San Francisco to one of the crucial events in the development of the art that would one day make fortunes for such as Gipsy Rose Lee: she allowed herself to be bound to Mazeppa's back for the grande finale, clothed in nothing but a pair of pink tights.

This attempt to bring realism into art stirred up a violent pro-and-con furor—gratifying box-office receipts, but also wrath from conservative customers who labeled her bouncing seminude charms the height of indecency.

> Her exhibitions [howled one critic,] are immodest and overdrawn caricatures, unfit for the public eye; degrading to the drama whose temples they defile; and a libel upon woman whose sex is hereby depraved and whose chastity is corrupted.

What Menken may have been as an actress is hard to determine. Her theatrical talents were overshadowed by her gaudy reputation as a fast woman careless of husbands, an equestrienne, and a forerunner of burlesque queens. But she certainly contributed to bringing circus onto the stage as much as Rowe and his agonized Sylphide contributed to the contrary movement of bringing melodrama to the sawdust ring.

When circus improvements up to Eastern standards—gilded bandwagons, acrobats, bareback dramatics, and free shows for school children with greased-pole climbing contests (a new suit of clothes for the winner!)—failed to pull circus business out of the economic quagmire, Wilson's Circus decided to cash in on the Californian's traditional longing to see the elephant. Shrewdly Wilson introduced a truly mammoth pair, named in honor of English royalty: Victoria and Albert.

Victoria and Albert were instantly adored by a public bored with mere horses. Children especially loved them. It was a memorable day in Stockton when Victoria and Albert were caught taking a swim in the slough. Youngsters piled down the banks in squealing herds and splashed happily in the tepid water, in the very shadow of the mild gray beasts. Victoria and Albert continued to wallow in the cooling mud, with a royally democratic tolerance of their splashing, shrieking co-bathers.

As far as is known, nineteenth century wits and half-wits did not attempt to promote a show in which Adah of the pink tights fame co-starred with Albert.

Nevertheless, before they said good-bye to misty San Francisco and sailed off into the sunset, Victoria and Albert had a real contribution to make to the history of the so-called legitimate theater. They performed on the stage of one of San Francisco's largest and sturdiest theaters in a play commissioned especially for them, *The Elephant of Siam*. Critics concluded their performance was well above the average of current acting talent.

It can be said without contradiction that this represented the peak development of horse opera in the noncowboy (or mammoth) sense.

Some years before theater became so chaotically extravagant and mammoth, California caught its first glimpse of an actress who wove in and out of show business throughout the middle of the decade. But if she had any part in soothing and civilizing the frontiersman, it could be only by reverse action: she aroused all conventional souls to cry, "Purify the theater." Still she is remembered when elephants, excursions, temperance leaders, society *grandes dames* and all the antlike army of civilizers and organizers who changed California's style of living are individually forgotten.

CHAPTER *18*

Caroline and the Countess

IN YEARS TO COME, THE CARNIVAL THEATER WORLD OF CALIFORNIA WOULD OFTEN BE STARRED WITH EXOTIC SEMITITLED CREATURES BLOWING into town on a purple wind of glamour and sensationalism, mysterious females with tattered bits of history clinging to them like secondhand scraps of royal banners.

But in 1853 California was having its first Countess and taking it rather like a schoolboy going to his first meeting with a fabuous lady of the demimonde.

Maria Dolores Eliza Rosanna Gilbert called herself a danseuse and played at being an actress. Actually she never acted any role but the one great role she had created for herself: the role of Lola Montez. She was born in Ireland of a parentage so confused that one could hardly blame her for choosing to be Spanish, though her predominant stock was probably Irish. She never denied—and in her characteristic choice of romantic black gown with white decolletage rather encouraged—the rumor of a left-handed descent from the poet Byron, though this relationship was actually of temperament, not of blood. At eighteen, to escape a forced marriage to an older man, she eloped with a British soldier, went to India and very soon divorced him. She was already creating and perfecting her lifelong role: tempestuous, temperamental, violent, dangerous, irresistible, invincible—completely a law unto herself.

What woman actually lived behind this self-image which she painted with such artistry and forced upon her public so vividly that no one who saw the picture forgot it? This remains an enigma. It is fair to guess that the temperamental traits from which she built the image were chosen from traits basic to her true nature. But it is fair to guess also that she was driven to do what she did, and be what she appeared to be, by a tragic thirst for attention, power and self-realization. Attention and power she gained in great measure; self-realization, probably never; and nothing she won ever satisfied that ruinous deep thirst.

She loved, or appeared to love, a great many men with an intensity which drove her into many difficult situations. Actually it is questionable whether this egocentric spirit was ever really capable of love. But the romantic urge which catapulted her into one affair after another made her for her time a symbol of the grand passion handled in the grand manner. And, handled in this manner, it served to cut her lovers down one after another—by accident, by suicide, by fighting—as surely as if she herself had leveled her own cherished dueling pistol at their hearts.

The French novelist Dumas *père*, who was her friend in Paris, took note of this coincidence long before the list of ruined men was complete, and commented that Lola had "the evil eye" for all who loved her. One of the most notable of her lovers, musician Franz Liszt, was too powerful to be harmed by her, although she broke up his common-law relationship with a mistress who had borne his children.

Once, after a quarrel with Lola, Liszt was said to have slipped quietly out of their hotel room, locking the door behind him, and down the back stairs of the hotel. He left no forwarding address. Lola was locked in for hours, beating hysterically upon the door. Yet she came back to him time after time, for a month this year, a couple of months the next.

Other lovers were not so invincible. Her most famous protector, Louis, King of Bavaria, lost in her service nothing more valuable than his self-respect and the devotion of his people.

It was because of King Louis that Lola was known as Countess of Lansfeld. This title she won fairly enough in the lists of Eros and wore with considerable distinction during the years when she was more than a kept woman to the aging king. She was the inspiration of his poetry, his political advisor and triumphant power behind the throne. Her romantic leanings towards political democracy helped push into effect certain reforms and caused her to be praised in other countries as a great fighter for democracy. Naturally there was a strong reaction. A growing important political force, sparked especially by the Jesuits, conspired to overthrow her and eventually succeeded. Louis swore he would never give her up, but in the end he banished her as a witch, sending her to a mesmerist to have the evil spirits driven from her much as today we would put a recalcitrant rebel into the hands of the psychotherapist. By this act of cowardice the king won for himself six more weeks of rule. At the end of that time, worn out by the whole struggle, he abdicated in favor of his son and spent the rest of his life devoting himself to art.

Lola tried a second legal marriage to an impressionable Englishman much younger than herself, saw it annulled by the husband's outraged aunt on the grounds that her divorce had been only partial, and left England abruptly for the United States.

She had not been able to draw into herself artistic talent from her contact with Liszt; she had gained no literary ability from acquaintance with Dumas and a real attachment to a young French

179

editor who left her by means of death in a duel; and the political power she had temporarily sucked into the insatiable quicksands of her ego was lost when her king exiled her. She was an indifferent dancer and a terrible actress, but there was no way for her to capitalize upon herself except to display Lola Montez on the stage. In this profession she passed rapidly through the large cities of the United States, experiencing over and over the same sequence of events: initial enthusiasm, riotous welcome, disappointment, fiasco, failure. People came to the theater in droves to see the king's mistress, the witch of Bavaria; they stayed to discover she could not dance or act and then, curiosity satisfied, they deserted her. She was a notorious personage, not a stage personality, and the sharp repeated up-and-down graph of her success and failure was exactly what that fact would predict.

Her record in California was similar except that the ups and downs were sharper. There were qualities in her nature—qualities she emphasized for theatrical effect—that vibrated in phase with the qualities of gold-rush California: adventurousness, wildness, effrontery, courage and hatred of convention. Therefore, the personality of Lola appealed more deeply, and was tolerated more widely, in the free society of the golden state. But there were other qualities in her romantic self-image which ran more against the grain of Californians than of milder, softer people. A California audience loved broad humor; it expected to laugh at, and with, its entertainers as it laughed at, and with, itself. When it turned its tolerant amusement and crude sense of burlesque upon Lola, the California audience outraged her in her most vulnerable spot: her intense seriousness about the magic, mystic properties of her beloved creation, Lola Montez. Their shocked indignation she could have taken as a tribute; their laughter was ruinous to her. And Californians, in turn, could not understand a woman constitutionally incapable of laughing at herself.

180

Lola was a dark and vivid creature, with coppery black hair and a red voluptuous mouth; a woman whose slender rounded body hardly fitted with her reputation for horsewhipping her enemies, but whose fierce blue-black eyes fitted that reputation all too well. While she occasionally attempted roles in ordinary plays, usually she starred as Lola in the autobiographical epic *Lola Montez in Bavaria*. Her characteristic dance, which she performed on every possible occasion, was the notorious spider dance, copied from Fanny Essler's Tarantula, but branded with the basic personality of Lola more completely than any other act she performed.

Eyewitness accounts described her as dashing onto the stage like an Arabian mare, forceful and fiery, dressed in a multicolored costume not overly long in the skirt. She then wandered into a spider's nest and began to dance, the cobwebs entangling her ankles, the spiders beginning to colonize about her legs. Spiders crawled up her, taking unwarrantable liberties, but "one jumps to the conclusion that she is enough for them. It is Lola versus the spiders. After a series of examinations and shaking of dresses, she . . . apparently stamps daylight out of the last ten thousand . . . and glides from the stage, overwhelmed with applause, and smashed spiders . . . cobwebs and glory."

A less starry-eyed account, couched in the semiliterate jargon that passed for humor, gives a picture both of the dance itself and of the rather wry amusement with which this performance—considered by Lola to be the height of her Art—was received in California:

> Spriggins told me there was something peculiar about the Countess' dancing. There is, Mr. Editor. . . . Spriggins said the Spider Dance was to represent a girl that commences dancing and finds a spider on her clothes and jumps about to shake it off. If that's it, Mr. Editor, then in the first part of the dance I guess she must see the spider up on the

ceiling, and that it's in trying to kick the cobwebs down that she gets the spider upon her clothes. She kicked up and she kicked around in all directions, and first it was this leg and then it was the other and her petticoats were precious short, Mr. Editor, on purpose to give her a fair chance. [The kicking match between Lola and the spiders caused this bashful observer to put his hat over his eyes and just peep over the brim, and then a man upstairs began hollering "Hey! Hey!" and soon everybody was yelling, and] I took my hat down from my eyes to see what was up. If the Countess wasn't crazy, I don't know what on earth was the matter with her. She seemed to get so excited like, that she forgot that there was any men at all about there. . . . [At that point the audience began stamping on the floor so roughly that our shy observer rushed out of the hall, afraid] the house would come down, or she'd take her dress right off, and I couldn't stand it.

"Why, it is nothing to be afraid of when you get used to it," says Spriggins, "and you went away before you saw all."

But, Mr. Editor, I saw more than I wanted to, and I ain't used to it—that's a fact.

News of the spider dance went around California like a hot tip on the ponies, and miners rushed to see whether or not they could get used to it. Some of them blushed and went home to make up a folk jingle in which the notorious bandit Joaquin Murietta reproved her:

> Joaquin through the mountains was advancing
> When he saw Lola Montez dancing,
> When she danced the spider dance
> He was bound to run her off—

Actually, if they had ever met, Lola and the bandit would probably have been great friends. They had a lot in common.

As the novelty of Lola's daring wore away, Californians took a second look at the self-made enigma, the passionate sphinx, the poseuse smiling sadly at sorrows no one could know and racked by epic rages, and with this second look California humor began to flicker like summer lightning around the stark and phony tragedy queen. And the person to encourage and channel this lightning was a comedy queen whose dominance over the California stage Lola had challenged: Caroline Chapman.

When Lola exploited the legend of her revolutionary activities in her autobiographical play; when Lola danced a crazy dance with great artistic seriousness; when Lola overestimated her thespian talent by taking several roles in a single play (no one of which turned out to be anything but Lola)—she presented a fine opening to one of the wittiest, saltiest and gayest women who ever toured the diggings and jolted bored miners into startled laughter. Caroline Chapman wasn't pretty and she wasn't young, but she had a piquant sense of humor that fitted exactly with the broad, antisentimental, semicruel wit of the forty-niners. These were the people who could see very well when the king had no clothes on and were ready to shout it to the world no matter how uncultured it might make them look.

"Our Caroline" was reigning spirit of the Chapman clan. The Chapmans were a close-knit family of gypsy-wild characters reputed to have second sight, to talk over the heads of outsiders with lightning-like finger language, and to stem from family theatrical tradition running clear back to Shakespeare's day. Coming from England in the 1820's, they had promoted the first Mississippi showboat because a boat was the only thing large enough to hold the whole family, and because all of them loved fishing second only to acting. Their California showboat steamed up and down the Sacramento River while the Chapmans diligently fished over the side, script in one hand and pole in the other. Their queen bee Caroline was the toast of the California stage when Lola invaded—a position she saw no reason to relinquish.

Now it was not Lola versus the imaginery spiders. It was romantic, Byronesque, solemn Lola versus a real actress with a razor-edge sense of the ridiculous. In the duel that followed, the outcome was never in doubt. Lola was the fairest of fair game for such as Caroline.

When the Countess took three parts in the same play, Caroline took seven parts in the skit *Actress of All Work*. Between acts she performed a broad burlesque of the spider dance, appropriately titled Spy-Dear, and stressing exhibitionism. These shows she and her brothers followed with a performance of Dr. Robinson's newest satire, *Who's Got the Countess*, in the course of which everyone from stars to prompter took a poke at Lola. Robinson, as the prompter, got a good many laughs out of byplay mimicking Lola's frequent inability to remember her lines. Finally Caroline's brother Billy presented his own version of the dance of the spiders, so outdoing the women that a customer wrote a choleric letter to the papers speaking "in plain terms of the conduct of a man who danced in female attire in one of our theaters. . . . The writer, who was accompanied by his wife and daughter, says that he never witnessed a more disgusting spectacle on the stage, and that it was a deliberate insult to a large audience."

Letters to editors began to fly fast and free from people on both sides of the fight. Lola was definitely getting the worst of it. But she eased out from under as smoothly as one of her own big black spiders: she surprised everybody by getting married again.

This strategic retreat into domesticity involved the temporary use of a young newspaperman, Pat Hull. They were married in a quiet dignified ceremony at the Mission Dolores and went on a stormy honeymoon to Monterey and then Sacramento. According to some stories, she lost her temper with Pat sufficiently to throw his belong-

184

ings out of the second-story window of the Golden Eagle Hotel, thus terminating the marriage during the honeymoon. Other accounts have him continuing in her company for some months longer.

Chased off the San Francisco stage by Our Caroline, Lola campaigned to capture Sacramento. But her reputation had preceded her, and valley audiences were crude. Her most energetic dances brought hearty guffaws from the provincials of the interior. "Apes!" she cried at them, and characteristically challenged the whole audience to a duel: "Give me your pants and take my petticoats. You're not fit to be called men. Lola Montez is proud to be what she is. But you, who have not the courage to fight a woman who scorns every one of you . . . !"

This called for a shower: rotten eggs and fruit. The manager tearfully begged the co-star, violinist Miska Hauser (who had attracted Lola's fancy about the time she married Hull) to "go out there and fiddle a few charms to soothe the savage beasts." Trembling, Hauser fiddled. The audience screamed, "Let's just have Hauser! No more Lola!" Lola heard this and came furiously dancing back. Now the spectators began tearing up the chairs and throwing them at the stage. Hauser fiddled and beseeched; Lola obstinately kept on trying to finish her dance. She had to be escorted to her hotel by a bodyguard of gallants with drawn pistols to protect her from threatened lynching.

At midnight a crowd gathered around her hotel with tin buckets and old kettles "for the purpose of giving her a Pike County serenade, which they did up in good style, which called forth the lady" who gave an encore on her previous curtain speech and was answered by terrific groans from the crowd.

Lola was a queen, and queens are not amused—not ever—by *lèse-majesté*.

The next night she got a much more appreciative reception from another Sacramento audience and also consented to apologize for her

185

own part in the uproar. This kiss-and-make-up scene did not prevent a heckling editor from asserting the audience that night was filled with a claque of Lola's friends. Raging all over again, Lola challenged that editor to a duel: he could fight her with her own precious pistol set, or he could select one of two pills in a box, one of which was lethal and the other harmless, Lola of course to swallow the other. The editor wisely refused to play Russian Roulette with Lola in any form. This story was headlined by unsympathetic newspapers, "Pistols or Pizen?"

Most of her glamour now stripped from her in large pieces, the Countess headed for the hills. In 1853 she settled down in Grass Valley (some accounts say Pat Hull was there with her for a while) where she bought a demure white house and turned to raising fancy flowers and taming grizzly cubs. Besides grizzlies and cacti, she collected herself a salon of stray actors, poets, child actresses like Lotta Crabtree whom she coddled, taught and influenced, and comical drunks. It was the Bohemia of the diggings. The little town puzzled what to do with her, finally gave her a certain measure of tolerance and guarded acceptance. California always took great pride in its eccentric characters, even as a highly respectable university might point with self-approbation at its single Socialist.

Lola wearied of the quiet life in 1855 and sailed very suddenly for Australia with a suite of followers collected from her Grass Valley clique, including an actor named Follett (or Folland) who left wife and children behind in San Francisco.

A year later Lola returned in a haze of new stories about duels, affairs and horsewhipping episodes, but without the deserting actor. He jumped overboard on the return trip. This reportedly was a real blow to Lola. Her brief 1856 venture on the San Francisco stage seemed to indicate her fire was burning low. She impulsively took to playing engagements *with* the Chapmans, perhaps hoping in that way

186

to hush their ridicule. It didn't work—they taunted her to her face. They probably did not intend cruelty; that was just the characteristic manner of Chapmans and California theatricals. Even when she made the royal gesture—sold her jewels at auction and gave the proceeds to the orphaned children of the suicidal actor—the Chapmans pursued her like Nemesis with a new burlesque: *A Trip to Australia, or Lola Montez on the Fanny Major.*

But Caroline Chapman too was wearing out, and the sporting instinct of the audience caused them to decide Lola had been whipped enough and to come roundly to her defense.

Lola refused to defend herself. During her last brief months in San Francisco, before she went East to die a few years later in New York City, she was busy playing a new role. She was quiet, rapt, reserved. She strode the streets of San Francisco in a dark cloak, brooding, with a fierce white parrot perched upon her shoulder. She drew about her no coterie of jesters and vagabonds, but vague pious people earnestly dedicated to spiritualism.

In a tiny cottage trimmed with iron gingerbread, Lola fed her tropical birds and welcomed her eccentric new friends with her old hospitality; and there, when the parrots were hooded and the protecting dark drew in about her cottage, Lola Montez held not salons but séances.

Her final role, in New York, she played offstage: it was that of the penitent Magdalene. With this she rounded out nearly thirty years of incessant acting upon the stage of the world. The part she created and played all those long years—like a richly woven and brilliantly styled ball gown—both hid and revealed the woman born Eliza Gilbert. To what extent it revealed her, to what extent it hid her, no one can say.

San Francisco did not forget her. But the kaleidoscope of show business went right on turning without her, as if she had never existed.

CHAPTER *19*

Pugilists and Ponies

As TODAY YOU CAN CHOOSE BETWEEN SPENDING YOUR SATURDAY AFTER-
NOON AT A MOVIE, A CONCERT, OR A FOOTBALL GAME, SO ALSO IN GOLD-
rush California there were shows that were specifically sporting events.

But the meaning of the word "sport" was not in that period so
firmly nailed to athletics. If you asked a forty-niner what "sport"
meant to him, he wouldn't reply with "World Series" or "Army-Navy
game," and he most certainly wouldn't refer to anything so mild as
billiards. "Sport" meant a water-front character, a fireman, a race-
track gambler, the rough fellow in the loud plaid trousers.

Although spectator sports were progressing, as were individual
competitive sports, they had a long way to go before reaching a point
where they would share honors with the eagle and the hot dog as an
American trademark.

Compared to conditions today, sports were haphazard and unorganized. Many of them still had an unsavory connotation. Spectator
sports were even more inseparably bound to gambling than they are
now. Prize fighting was still illegal in most states, and it was highly
radical of the San Francisco Jockey Club even to consider a bylaw
permitting "nice" women, properly escorted by husbands or brothers,
to attend a horse race. If parasols did show up at the track, their
bearers sat stiffly apart in a special bleacher stand and bore the stares
and leers of the crowd. The restriction—like the ban on women in
saloons—did not of course apply to not-nice women.

Women were banned from the track because of its close connection with gambling. They were kept out of prize-fight audiences for this reason and also because, while the prize fight had improved somewhat since colonial days when men used to bite off ears and gouge out eyes, it was still a brutal and lawless exhibition. Obviously the trend during the fifties was for young men to take out more and more of their competitive spirit by backing horses or pugilists, and less by using each other for target practice. But this did not necessarily indicate a civilizing influence or a softening of the crude male spirit.

For Californians whose taste in fighting ran to bloody slugging matches rather than duels or bullfights, there were numerous scraps between battered lesser pugilists, many amateur boxing matches and spontaneous scuffles, and occasional highly touted exhibitions by two nationally famous professional battlers: Yankee Sullivan and James Heenan.

Yankee Sullivan, national champion until 1853, came to California in 1841 when he was released from a term in Australia's penal colony. He drifted about the state giving exhibition matches during the early years of the rush, and it was here that he earned the nickname "Yankee" by wearing the American flag for a girdle while he fought.

The other major fighter, James Heenan, destined to win the world's championship from an Englishman in 1860, also gained his *nom de guerre* in the gold country. When his hunt for nuggets proved profitless, Heenan took a job with a steamship line in Benicia, where he worked between bouts in the ring. In his later famous years he was known as the "Benicia Boy" because of this brief interval of honest toil in that locality.

The Benicia Boy entertained the miners and won fame in the prize ring. He won fame equally for his brief round in the wedding ring with Adah Isaacs Menken, the seminude rider of Mazeppa, which went two or three months and ended in a knockout victory for Adah. Heenan stood six-foot-two in fighting garb and was compared to Apollo and Hercules; his Irish brogue, winning smile, and ardent glance accordingly "made her heart, falsely thought to be moribund, go pit-a-pat." But this wasn't the whole story: he not only lacked refinement, tenderness, and brains, but he also gambled, drank, and ran around with wild women. Furthermore Adah had absent-mindedly forgotten to divorce her previous husband before she married Heenan. But the short-lived match was not a complete loss for either contender: each cashed in on the publicity of the other.

At the encounters of these and lesser pugilists, about the only law was "anything goes." The Marquis of Queensberry rules were an unhatched egg in the nest of the future. There was no code worth mentioning. Professional fighters were usually riffraff, often ex-convicts. The spectacle of a fighter winning publicity for his attention to Shakespeare would have bewildered and shocked them. Fights were looked upon with such raised eyebrows even in the early wide-open period that one contest was held near the Mission Dolores at 1:45 A.M., with a furtive secrecy quite in contrast to the open acceptance of bullfights and duels. A few years later, a Sonora fight that lasted for an hour and a half of ruthless slugging aroused a violent public outcry. There was no limit to the number of rounds and very little tendency to call it a draw on account of injuries: the rule was nearly "kill or be killed."

The attitude of the period shows up clearly in the statement of one journal that it would never support legislation against drinking or gambling, but prize fighting should be forbidden by law as it was in other states. "How heartless and depraved must be those who brought these two unfortunate persons together to fight for *rowdy fame* and

190

paltrey gold; they who were heretofore strangers to each other."

Here is the key to the puzzle: Why should Californians cry out against prize fighting when they tolerated so much private brawling? Obviously it was because the fighters were strangers to each other and had nothing against each other. Therefore, the whole thing was so incredibly cold-blooded! It was understandable to put a bullet through the ribs of someone who insulted your girl or insinuated that you had cheated at monte, but it was barbarous and uncivilized for two characters to fight with no better motive than publicity and money.

So while the law sporadically and reluctantly moved to crack down on professionals, amateur fights—whether engaged in to satisfy a grudge or to release excess energy or out of general high-spirited competitiveness—passed with a mild "tut tut" from good citizens and enjoyed the enthusiastic support of wharfside toughs. Such was a typical incident reported in the *Alta California*:

> Two sailor-looking men, full of strychnine, indulged themselves in the recreation of attempting to knock each other down, on Kearny street, corner of Jackson, about one o'clock yesterday morning. They would "square off" at each other and at a "pass," whether hit or not, one would fall and the other tumble on top of him. . . . Then they would stagger to their feet and after a brief war of words try another round. . . . Thus they continued to fight to the great amusement of a crowd of encouraging spectators for some fifteen minutes.

Naturally the incoming troupes of Sweet Betseys strongly disapproved the spectacle of grown men engaging in such juvenile, barbaric amusements, and slowly they made their influence felt. Fighting, not yet formalized into an acceptable sport, was pushed more and more into the off-limits of clandestine stag activities.

The competitive spirit found a more approved and wholesome

outlet in many kinds of races. Most of them merged in various proportions the elements of spectator sport, personal participation and participation by gambling.

Personal competition found a preferred outlet in foot races, though these also enjoyed a wide audience. They were a fairly common Sunday amusement in the mines. One of the earliest was a tortoise-and-hare business between two miners who raced from Downieville Buttes down twelve miles of stony trail to Downieville. The prize was a purse of five hundred dollars. The more ambitious contestant started out at a good hard sprint over the boulders and around the pines. He kept it up for two or three miles and then, worn out but refusing to rest, stumbled blindly over a precipice and crashed down a steep ravine. Friends picked him up and carried him to the camp hospital, while his less eager rival dogtrotted comfortably along and finished the stretch at leisure.

Gold-town foot races, either between two star performers or free-for-all style, were widely publicized and well attended. At the free-for-alls, each runner put up a hundred dollars as entrance fee, and the rule was "winner take all"—except fifty dollars for the second-place man. The main wager on a race might vary from a thousand dollars in gold to twenty-five dollars in cigars. Of course the total of sums exchanged in side bets added up to many times as much as the principal wager. Spectators came from all over the neighboring country whenever one of these races was held, and enthusiasm was sometimes excessive—as in the case of a reporter who returned from a well-attended mountain track meet to record in the *Golden Era* that the winner did the hundred-yard dash in eight seconds! (Downhill, perhaps?)

Horse racing, with regular tracks and definite seasons, came into prominence as early as 1850 and was well established by the mid-fifties. The fact that it was already a favorite sport of the native Spanish Californians, notoriously rapid men with a horse, eased the way for racing. Unlike the other prime sport of the natives, bullfighting, horse racing strengthened with time into an institution. One of the best tracks was frugally revamped from the bullfight arena near the Mission Dolores when bullfighting lost favor. Most of the races were trotting matches between two or three horses "to harness," the victor winning two out of three heats. But Californians worked out their own variations, sometimes racing a trotter against a pacer, or harnessing horses in the same race to different vehicles—one "to skeleton," another "to wagon and driver," and the third to the standard light racing sulky. Or they experimented with odd lengths: in 1857 trotters General Taylor and Rattler ran in harness a thirty-mile race. The General won by four minutes with a time of one hour and forty-nine minutes. These marathons were too hard on the ponies to become common events.

Often chauvinism added a fillip to equine competition. The larger issue could be Yankee-versus-Mexican or California-versus-effete East. When California's own Wake-up Jake raced Boston colt Attila, members of the state legislature were sadly puzzled how to get off for the race until one pious gentleman recalled that the event was scheduled for Good Friday. The Senate passed a resolution to adjourn on that day for religious observances. As a result, the good gentlemen of the legislature were able to give Wake-up Jake the necessary moral support and he won easily, thus confirming all present in their faith that horses (as well as yachts, nuggets, and fruit) grew much bigger and better in the golden state.

This faith was unwarranted. The speeds set by California's Daniel Webster, Fred Johnson and General Taylor compared poorly with the records of Eastern first-raters. While the trotting record for the mile stood at 2:17½, the best speeds of California thoroughbreds fell in the low 2:30's, and even 2:47—set by the winner at a two-thousand-dollar San Francisco race in 1858—was considered fast time. Soon Leland Stanford changed this with his Palo Alto farm.

If the chauvinistic split was between gringo and ranchero, the American animal often appeared the better physical specimen. Easter Monday of 1850, when Pio Pico staged a return engagement to win revenge against Mr. Hudspeth's American nag who had previously beaten him at Sonoma, an observer claimed Hudspeth's horse looked like a pampered sire, while Pico's resembled a creature just recovering from influenza. This race (again the joy of the politicians, this time San Jose's famous "legislature of a thousand drinks") * was to be run for a ten-thousand-dollar purse over a five-hundred-vara course. (A vara was slightly less than a yard.) The course was straight, along two separate parallel tracks, located about four feet apart, and was not staked or roped off. The whole town of San Jose—politicians moving among them busily canvassing votes—turned out to line these trails: foot people inmost, then horsemen, people in buggies forming the third line. The lines kept breaking ranks, making it necessary for friends of the principals to ride along forcing order—Spanish very polite, Yankees swearing insolently. Child-sized jockeys, bootless and spurless, were set bareback upon the horses. The horses wore nothing but a narrow surcingle, inside which the jockeys could thrust their knees to help them hold on.

When order was finally restored, the horses were led to the post. Tensely silent, the people waited. Almost all of them had bet heavily on the race. The pistol sounded, and the horses were off, thundering past the toes of pushing, swaying spectators, setting a fast pace down the narrow track. And the beautiful Yankee horse won again. The Spanish

---

* California's first state legislature convened in San Jose. Later the citizens voted on which city should be the capital, and Sacramento won after an acrimonious contest.

shrugged and turned away; the Yankees indulged in a howling uproar, crude as usual: "I knowed we would whip them damned tawneys!"

Race tracks served a particularly useful social function as trial grounds for tests of speed between Volunteer Fire Companies. These volunteer firemen were a rough and colorful part of every nineteenth century city's street scene: professionally brave, egotistically gaudy, hopelessly rowdy. They were notorious for racing to fires through the streets, often disabling rival engines in passing in order to make sure of beating the other company to the fire. To work off this rivalry under less critical circumstances, fire companies staged races on the local tracks which safely satisfied the need to prove superiority. Under this system, nobody's house burned down while the fireboys fought in the street for the honor of getting there first.

Sometimes the exuberant firemen carried their competition to its logical extreme: taking the horses' place, they dragged the heavy horse-carriages around the track, fifteen to a team, the teams changing off relay fashion.

Unfortunately carriage racing was not a purely spectator sport confined to the track. Many a young man went down to a livery stable, rented the fastest horse and the frailest buggy, and lurked on a downtown street corner waiting for somebody else with similar equipment. Upon catching sight of each other, the two speed demons would charge off down the street, lashing their horses, jockeying for position, oblivious to traffic and pedestrians, upsetting applesellers and newsboys and threatening the lives of everyone in sight. Montgomery Street (San Francisco's Wall Street) was the favored racecourse of amateur charioteers. Here not only peddlers but also captains of finance were frequently grazed by the high spidery wheels and flying hooves of the spiritual ancestors of our hot-rod boys.

The police department, lacking the true sporting spirit, called it "furious driving," and hauled the gay young blades into court whenever they could catch up with them, which wasn't very often.

This kind of racing could not properly be called a spectator sport, as spectators were usually in a poor position to enjoy it. Quite the opposite was true of regattas. Everyone crowded down to the shores of the Bay when one of these water festivals took place. Bands played, mothers and children crowded the water front along with their men, to watch the graceful yachts fly across the whitecaps like giant gulls. And it was holiday all over town.

Public sporting events were still almost entirely confined to various kinds of fighting and racing. Team sports as we know them were in their infancy and did not as yet provide much of a show for the money. Schoolboys played ball on the Plaza, and everywhere on sand lots and mountain clearings men relaxed by throwing a ball around, but ball games were casual and relatively unorganized. During the fifties a few sport clubs held regular cricket matches. It was not until the end of the decade that the Great American Game finally began nosing out the cricketeers.

In 1860, twenty years after its origin, baseball went West. It was introduced in San Francisco by the Eagle Base-ball Club, modeled on the gentlemanly clubs of the East, playing against a printers' outfit called the Em-Quad Club. The Fourth of July match between the Eagles and the Sacramento Base-ball Club was the state's first intercity contest.

As entertainment, sporting events were meager and undeveloped compared to the rich overexuberant flamboyance of the San Francisco theater. Sport had comparatively little to offer as a spectacle. But individual participation games of all kinds, strenuous and quiet, flourished in every corner of the state, from the back alleys of Chinatown to the crooked canyon trails of the mining camps.

196

CHAPTER *20*

Clubs and Clean Fun

Wʜᴇɴ ᴄᴏɴᴛᴇᴍᴘᴏʀᴀʀʏ ʜɪsᴛᴏʀɪᴀɴ ᴊᴏʜɴ ʜɪᴛᴛᴇʟʟ ᴄʟᴀɪᴍᴇᴅ ɪɴ 1860 ᴛʜᴀᴛ ʙɪʟʟɪᴀʀᴅs ᴡᴀs ᴛʜᴇ ғᴀᴠᴏʀɪᴛᴇ ᴀᴍᴜsᴇᴍᴇɴᴛ ᴏғ ᴄᴀʟɪғᴏʀɴɪᴀɴs, anybody who has followed the long rowdy catalogue of things forty-niners did with their spare time will call it a hasty overgeneralization. But truly enough, in every rickety "hotel" of every tiny village, billiard tables and bowling alleys were as indispensable as spittoon and bar.

A hotel would bunk all its patrons in one big room; it could provide a common toothbrush and no plumbing, but it could not stay in business without billiard equipment. The "gentleman's parlor" of such a hotel was the Californian's first club: a bare ugly room with an iron stove squatting in the center of it surrounded by benches and chairs. Here the quieter citizens gathered on winter evenings, rocking their chairs back on two legs, as many as possible crowding their feet onto the stove's hot fender, chewing their inevitable quids of tobacco, endlessly talking and gossiping. According to an Englishman, their talk "almost uniformly turns upon the illness under which the speaker last suffered." After a while somebody would pull out a pack of tobacco-stained cards, and chair legs would come down with a thump as club members rearranged themselves for a lazy game of poker or euchre. Chess, the dime novel, and chewed-up newspapers several weeks old also helped the parlor habitués endure their lifeless leisure.

And two billiard tables placed near the big stove would keep the hotel loafers happily out of mischief for hours at a time. The same snobbish Englishman wrote of Hangtown's "billiard saloon": "Those not playing line the benches on each side of the tables, and from thence completely saturate the floor with the tobacco juice which they dislodge upon it." (English travelers were notoriously incapable of seeing the Yankee heart of gold through the spray of tobacco juice.)

The gentleman's parlor—as well as later more formal clubs, Debating Societies, Hibernian Societies, Lodges and Temples—was a sanctum sanctorum of masculinity: no women allowed. On the other hand, men were welcome in the women's parlor. Men no sooner got their women to the gold country than they began barricading themselves into small corners where the stag existence could go on without petticoat interference. They wanted women, all right, but they believed in zoning: woman in the kitchen, at the dance, beside the cradle; *no* women in the billiard parlor, the saloon, the bowling alley.

From the beginning, bowling alleys were almost as common as saloons. Dame Shirley wrote of Rich Bar:

> The rolling on the bowling alley never leaves off for ten consecutive minutes at any time during the twenty-four hours. It is a favorite amusement at the mines, and the only difference that Sunday makes is, that then it never leaves off for *one* minute.

But though such places were declared by ironbound custom sacred to men only, women of "a certain type" did appear in them nevertheless. One of the things that made Grass Valley women draw their skirts aside when Lola Montez passed by was that Lola used to stroll into the local tenpin alley with a big cigar in her mouth, order the barkeeper to set up beer for the crowd, and bowl a few rounds with her bearded friends.

An even safer retreat, at first glance, was the men's gymnasium. The German immigrants, with their *Turnverein* societies, were largely responsible for establishing gym sports (as they were also for many

198

of the organizations devoted to music, such as San Francisco's Philharmonic Society and New Germania Concert Society). The Turners devoted most of their efforts to weight lifting and setting-up exercises; the most accomplished members gave tumbling exhibitions. From 1852 on, San Francisco had gymnasiums where biceps builders taught the "American, English and German styles" of calisthenics in halls equipped with "ladders, parallel bars, horizontal bars, chest machines, handles for somerset turning, clubs, dumb bells, springboard, rowing machines, and numerous other apparatus."

But even the gym did not remain sole property of male musclemen. One daring gym master, making a financial success of his classes for school children, ventured further and set up a special class where those of the female persuasion might decorously flex the muscles fashion never revealed them to possess.

Still, if you were desperate for escape, you could always take a hunting party into the wilds of the Sierras. Where wild animals crowded the villages and food was scarce, hunting and fishing were only partly sport—they were also in large measure, as on any frontier, a means of livelihood. At first no rules, no hunting season restrictions, applied. Hunters prowled diligently from the highest canyons to the sandy hills just outside San Francisco's city limits. Soon the Bay region and other conveniently reached ranges changed from a wild animal's paradise to normal city suburbs, with never a deer in sight.

Hunters were so enthusiastic, skillful, and hungry that laws had to be passed regulating the shooting of the antelope, elk and wild horses that ranged freely over the San Joaquin Valley. Around cities, objections started sooner: in 1849 people put up signs forbidding goat-shooting on Telegraph Hill. But while antelope and suburban goats came to be protected, there was still open season on grizzly bears, rattlesnakes, and other varmints.

By the end of the decade all the goats were gone from Telegraph

Hill; the small game had vanished from the dunes near the Bay; and San Franciscans had to resort to shooting galleries like other city dwellers, or take out their hunting zeal by organizing pigeon shootings in which live pigeons were sprung from a trap. By that time, however, a man's life was less dependent upon his speed with a six-shooter.

Anglers were also blessed with profusion in the early days. They might with profit throw out a line into almost any water. If a man went on an excursion steamer, he could fish over the edge; if he mined a mountain creek, he could hook his supper trout not far from his claim.

It was amazing the odd places people found to fish in. Once a thirsty gentleman rushed into a bar on Pacific Street wharf and demanded a brandy straight, "right now!" Said the barkeeper, "Wait a second, I've got a bite." The stranger said never mind the free lunch, all he wanted was a brandy straight, but quickly. The barkeeper shook his head and continued to concentrate behind the counter. A moment later he held up a large fish flopping at the end of the line he had been dangling through a hole cut in the floor behind the bar.

Summer sports and snow sports were equally casual and uncommercialized. When the weather was hot, people sought the old swimming hole in the nearest creek or slough. In the wintertime, the mountain people built snowmen, threw snowballs and went sleigh riding. Because mining drew such large populations into the high Sierras, a comparatively high percentage of Californians lived where snow fell. Those who dwelt in the snowless valley towns made expeditions to the snowfields as they do today, but there were no ski resorts. Skiing had as yet made no serious impression on the United States.

There was, however, one skier in California: Norway-born "Snow-shoe Thompson," who recalled the usefulness of the long narrow wooden runners of his native land and constructed them from

200

memory. When blizzards walled the gold camps in with snow, Snowshoe Thompson was able to penetrate with a rescue kit of food and supplies. In 1857 the transcontinental telegraph reached the Nevada side of the Sierras, and suddenly Thompson found that his exotic skill had slid him right into a steady job: keeping winter communications open between California and the Nevada terminal. No one but the skier could possibly negotiate the tremendous drifts and snow-buried trails of the California-Nevada crossing.

Californians regarded Thompson with as much awe as if he had suddenly sprouted wings and begun to fly. A few of the bolder spirits experimented with skis out of curiosity, but no one foresaw their possibilities. Not one of California's sharp-eyed promoters had sufficient foresight to exploit Thompson's special means of transportation as a sport and establish a ski lodge on the slopes of the Sierra Nevadas.

Skis and the old swimming hole are a long long way from monte and lansquenet. Private gambling of course went on in the hotel parlors, friendly games of euchre and seven-up. But quieter and gentler diversions were making their inroads. Libraries and reading rooms were opening up all over the state. By 1860 the February circulation record of San Francisco's Mercantile Library indicated the modest place that literary amusement was winning: novels, two hundred and sixty; biography, sixty; travel books, fifty-seven; history, forty-six; literary sketches and verse, thirty-four; scientific volumes, fifteen; works on religion, eight. Obviously the people who liked science (lectures on mesmerism) and concern for the spirit (table tipping) were not among the most book-minded.

Chess was as popular among the quiet souls as reading. Many forty-niners played chess even in the wide-open days. As the state settled down and reluctantly consented to behave in a civilized manner, chess clubs and chess fiends sprang up in every direction.

It's hard to believe a chess club would engage in chess by mail in those days of snail-paced and uncertain mail service, but the Chess and Literary Association of Shasta challenged Yreka's club to just such a long-distance tourney. Every time Wells Fargo Express galloped into town, the stage brought news of Yreka's latest move. The Shasta players then gathered about their board and ceremoniously moved Yreka's man as instructed. While Wells Fargo unloaded and picked up new packages, Shasta masterminds pondered their countermove, moved their knight cautiously forward, and sent word of the knight's progress back to Yreka by stage. Yreka's players took the message and went through the same operation.

The San Francisco Pioneer Chess Club held its first tournament in 1858. It was not confined to club members. Anyone in the state could enter if he wanted to pay the five-dollar entrance fee. For half price, those who were talented at giving advice could buy a season ticket to kibitz.

Chess gained so many addicts that by 1860 almost every newspaper carried a chess problem.

In 1859 the Board of Directors of the Mercantile Library Association found their activities were running afoul of the new blue laws the "conservative element" had effected in order to curb California's traditional fiesta Sundays. After due consideration and much worried scrambling about, after thorough checking with politician friends, the Board solemnly voted by a large majority that their chess rooms would not have to close on Sunday.

Chess, according to their verdict, was *not* a boisterous and unseemly sport.

CHAPTER *21*

The Cotillion Set

IF CITIZENS OF THE TOWN THAT ONCE BOASTED A PLAZA RIMMED WITH CONTINUOUS GAMBLING HELLS HAD TO PASS A RULE THAT CHESS WAS *not* a boisterous and unseemly sport, so also did men who once caroused in the fandango cellars with ladies of harlequin masque have to adjust to the social order of Sunbonnet Betsey.

The old order changeth: as wives, families and household goods jogged across mountains and plains to California, propriety invaded first the cities and finally even the Argonaut's fortress, the diggings. Newly arrived social arbiters took one shocked look around and settled grimly to the task of separating the sheep from the goats. In some amazed villages the social fabric altered almost overnight.

When the Weaverville season of 1853 opened with a grand New Year's Ball, Mrs. Edwards from New Orleans and her like-minded cronies determined to make the dance a completely proper affair. Therefore they invited "only *respectable ladies* (you have to cull them out here.)" Weaverville had a lot of women of various colors, ages, sizes and degrees of moral turpitude; but when the dowagers finished scrutinizing reputations, Weaverville and vicinity had only about thirty ladies left. Twenty-four of guaranteed eighteen-carat virtue managed to attend the ball.

On New Year's Eve, the chosen people rustled up in silk and satin, while men who had never been out of red flannel somehow begged, borrowed or stole dress coats and white vests. There, smelling only of lavender and other genteel scents, the ladies gathered in cliques according to nationality (French, Spanish and American) to shake their curls over the sad fate of the uninvited. Many a generous-hearted belle of former fandangoes found herself on the blacklist. Similarly in other towns, at other New Year's balls, other lists were going up, stamping "pure" and "respectable" like trademarks of triumphant Victorian womanhood upon the social calendar of the gold country.

Three years later, Weaverville was further sissified by the introduction of dancing school. The prospector had to put on a clean shirt and learn to twist his big feet through the stately patterns of society's dances. Throughout the diggings, dancing masters were nailing up their shingles, and for every one ridden out of town on a rail, there were a dozen who stayed and collected nuggets from sheepish customers anxious to please some haughty new arrival.

"They have a dancing school also in full feather, only think of that for the mines," wrote Franklin Buck to his sister. "Mr. Wilson and Miss Burbank (the 'Divine Lizzie') guide them through the mazes of the waltz and schottische. After ten o'clock the school closes and anyone paying one dollar for the music has the right to pitch in. The night I attended there were about forty gents and twenty ladies, quite a ball. Don't you think Weaverville has changed since I wrote to you in the year '52?" But Franklin—the man who stepped all over Madame Chabord's flounce and ripped half her skirt away—was no prize scholar at the new school. Though he found it had improved the men so "they could all go through a cotillion without making a botch of it," he had to admit "I found myself behind the times when they called a schottische a waltz, not having paid as much attention to this as to the saw mill lately." At this Fourth of July ball, promoters took in a thousand dollars at the bar and still nobody in the ballroom appeared really drunk.

During the fifties, dancing parties and public halls became numerous enough to draw from the fandango houses that part of the trade which merely wanted a place to dance. Among the most hightoned were San Francisco's Apollo Balls, held in a big bare loft on Pacific Street. This drafty hall, with its unfinished rafters streaming bright flags and strips of bunting, stood in the heart of a district notorious even then and soon to become the Barbary Coast. But it was the only place large enough for high society's major parties, and according to Amelia Neville its crude wooden bleachers supported the wealth and beauty and décolleté of the city.

At one of these Apollo Balls, Lucy Gwin, daughter of the state's number one politician William Gwin, was formally introduced to that Society in which her father was cutting such a slashing figure:

> Suddenly a couple swooped down the room, in the dance, turned and rushed back again at breakneck speed. It was Lucy Gwin, making her debut, assisted by Billy Botts. He was a small man, and Lucy Gwin towered above him, while her crinolines nearly hid him from view. But he kept the pace, and emerged triumphant. He was the best "fancy dancer" in society, and his speed in the redowa was terrific. He would race with high steps down the length of a room, pause for the turn with one foot pointed, and then race back again.

In San Francisco even blue bloods amused themselves with more strenuosity than stuffy propriety. The prize wasn't always to the swift, but fairly often it was. A great many of the most popular steps were fast and fancy: the gallopade, the tarantelle, the sicilian.

But dancing, while always energetic, didn't have to be that complicated. For the colt-footed fellow from the hills, there were always the tried and true combinations of jig, slide, and swing your partner: the square dance, or Kentucky hoedown. The polka was widely popular too. In addition to society's fashionable steps and standard Hoosier square dances, cosmopolitan San Francisco enjoyed new patterns contributed by the flourishing foreign elements. The Irish popularized jigs and breakdowns, Spanish the jota and bolero, and both Spanish and Germans encouraged that dangerous novelty, the waltz.

At a time when almost all dances, plain and elaborate alike, were on a community pattern like the square dances of today, the waltz was revolutionary. Here was a dance involving not a group, but a single couple, and this couple enjoyed freedom of the floor. Not part of a co-operative group, the pair could dance here, there, or in the corner. Worst of all, the waltz required a closer embrace than did other current steps, and a man could keep his same partner throughout the whole dance instead of trading off with somebody else every few steps.

This was dangerous. Naturally blue bloods, conservative frontiersmen, and mothers frowned upon the waltz, while daughters hastened to learn it. The waltz did not become very fashionable in the fifties, and was not favored either at "Pike County hoedowns" or really formal balls. Still it was rapidly becoming first choice at small informal parties, and it was almost the only style at plebeian family playgrounds with strong German influence like Russ's Gardens.

While the vulgar waltz infiltrated from below, the high-class contingent sometimes introduced a new dance style from above. When some lively San Francisco youngsters were stranded in the river on their way to a Sacramento Inaugural Ball (the steamer hit the Hog's Back sandbar and couldn't get off until the tide turned in the morning), they solved the problem of how to spend the night without sleeping quarters by learning the latest quadrille hit from London, the Lancers.

206

While Billy Botts whistled "Money Musk" and called figures, we balanced to the right, swung our partners, and all chassez-ed on the deck of the *New World*, in the Sacramento River. That night in Sacramento, when we formed a hollow square and went through the maneuvers, we stopped the ball.

That ball was stopped by something far more paralyzing than the antics of gay San Franciscans introducing a new dance. The party took place in the Sacramento Theater, on a temporary dance floor built out over the orchestra pit, as no other hall could be found large enough to accommodate the crowd. On ball night, as Sacramento crackled in the worst frost of the winter, the committee suddenly remembered there was no way to heat the theater.

By the time this fact occurred to them, it was too late to change the plans. Guests arrived and huddled wretchedly in their wraps until the music started. Ladies with fashionable bare white arms and throats shivered through the Grand March and then made a frantic dash for the cloakroom. The rest of the night "lumpy-looking dolmans and long fur-lined capes revolved heavily on the crowded floor," giving the party the festive look of high jinks among the Eskimos.

In the depression years toward the end of the decade, social reformers began berating frivolous females who heartlessly squandered on a ball gown a sum of money that would keep a poor family from starvation for a month. Cowed by these leftist mutterings, society inaugurated calico balls. No lady could get in if she wore anything more expensive than calico. (Sweet Betsey had started this style some years ago because calico was her best ball dress, but fashion had failed at that time to copy.) Each *grande dame* was supposed to donate to charity the money she would have spent on a new satin gown.

The fad was eagerly adopted by socialites anxious to combine an evening's fun with a chance to feel that Lady Bountiful glow. One such party netted shantytown sufferers hush money to the tune of eight hundred dollars.

In the eyes of luxury-loving San Franciscans, it was an amazing sight to see "some twelve hundred plain print calico crinolines bobbing up and down and gyrating in waltz and quadrille. No uncouth grating sound of silk flounces rubbing against broadcloth was heard." There were, of course, always ladies who "could not resist the temptation of appearing singular, and therefore went a step beyond calico, and robed themselves in gay ginghams and flaunting muslin."

Husbands and fathers were extremely enthusiastic about calico balls, once they had corrected a slight misunderstanding about the rules. At first a few fashion dictators ordered that men should carry calico handkerchiefs and wear calico neckties. At this sacrilege, such a thunder of horrified protest arose that managers quickly reversed their ruling: of course men might wear silk and satin in the usual places. Once this ridiculous perversion of the calico idea was scotched, men declared themselves delighted with the new fashion.

There were, of course, skeptics whose X-ray eyes presumed to see through calico: they murmured cynically about Marie Antoinette's milkmaids, or grumbled that this was just a trick to convince unwary bachelors that matrimony wasn't so expensive after all.

Depression or not, ball announcements thickened on the society pages of the papers, and lavish expenditures on entertainment continued about as usual among those members of the *bon ton* not currently embarrassed with bankruptcy proceedings. At the same time, for those who were not wealthy, the respectable family dance halls rose and prospered—innocent beer gardens and amusement-park dance floors, "unfashionable," but safe and modestly priced.

By 1860 the most aristocratic of San Franciscans had taken another step toward Victorian stuffiness. They were beginning to doubt the propriety of public halls. But social competition had set a precedent for extravagance in entertaining: balls had to be given on a certain munificent champagne-floating scale, or the host would lose status. Few social leaders could afford it. As a private affair, the grand ball was pricing itself out of the market. The elite would not settle for less, as a rule, and would no longer patronize communal balls because of the constant infiltration of the *nouveau riche* from below. But the level of society affected by this superrefinement was numerically unimportant.

While some blue bloods took a huffy attitude, and while the less rigid middle class enjoyed the flowering of public dance facilities, still the fandango houses throve on the back streets of the cities. But they had many rivals now, and the trend from dance cellar to cotillion was unmistakable.

The notorious "bal masque" itself was sometimes commandeered by nice people. One cannot imagine that the masquerade ball Mrs. Appleton gave in 1858 had anything but the name in common with the lusty brawls of '49:

> "Mrs. Appleton was a dark beauty and charming in manner. She was dressed as a gypsy; Mrs. Smith as Night; Miss Yontez as Morning; Miss Packwood as Morning Star; Miss Lily Eschols as Mary, Queen of Scots."

All they needed was Billy Botts as "the New Year." But this type-casting of the ebullient Billy took place at another event:

> One evening we had charades, [recalled social leader Amelia Neville] with "The Seasons" represented by men of the party. Hall McAllister was Spring with a wreath of artificial flowers on his head and a scarf draped over his black

broadcloth. Judge Hager in a toga, carrying a feather fan, was Summer. Autumn was represented by Arthur Godde-froy, who carried a pumpkin, and Cutler McAllister in an overcoat was Winter. Lieutenant McPherson, of the Presidio, wore a cotton-wool beard to suggest Father Time, and Billy Botts was the New Year with infant's cap and bib, carrying a rattle.

The McAllisters named in this catalogue of coy masculine cutups were members of the tribe famous in New York, where Ward McAllis-ter helped establish the "Four Hundred." They, along with Billy Botts and his rattle, belonged to a world far removed from the bawdy faro-bucking night country of the forty-niner—a world that was being slowly but inexorably superimposed upon the old, like a Victorian portrait being painted over the lascivious mural of Leda and her Olympian bird.

The lines of the old picture still showed, but they were growing fainter.

What was the Argonaut to think when he read in his paper about a Presbyterian church bazaar, with an auction where one could bid for aprons and hand-knit socks, and a censored substitution for a kissing booth: "The Post Office Department . . . dispensed a goodly array of billet-deux, some of which were flattering and some not so much so."

"I remember it distinctly," one forty-niner wrote of his first church bazaar in Nevada City, "and I pity the poor fellows that were beset by the ladies as I was." Miss Bowers kept the post office, and as soon as a fellow paid his two dollars entrance fee and got inside, she accosted him with news of a letter. Feeling young and flattered, he stepped over to her office and accepted it. Then "she said, in the sweet-est of womanly accents, 'Two dollars and fifty cents.' I paid. . . . When I opened it I found it to be written in Dutch or Indian, not a word of which could I make out." The naive victim complained.

" 'Dear me, how stupid I was,' said she; 'but here is your letter,' hand-ing me another.'" Two dollars and a half again, please. No sooner had the miner escaped this fair leech than he was further exploited by the lady who kept the scales. This female exclaimed over his thin pale look: "Have you been sick?" He thought not, but agreed to get weighed and see if he was actually losing. Not so—in fact he had gained five pounds. "Well, well, I was mistaken," said she smiling: "People are liable to be deceived. Two dollars, please." The miner paid and left, "fully agreeing . . . that people are liable to be deceived, particularly at a ladies' church bazaar. I had not been in the house more than an hour when my experience had cost me about thirty dol-lars. I don't remember how much the fair netted, but it was something enormous. The miners were captivated with the smiles of the la-dies . . . ; nor were the ladies sparing of their blandishments, so long as the miners' money held out. The gamblers, too, came in for their share, and got as handsomely fleeced as they ever fleeced a poor miner."

How was the forty-niner to believe his eyes when he saw the signs going up announcing lecture groups, literary clubs, debating societies and lyceums in the mines?

Even in 1852, Sonora was "very dull compared to what it used to be," wrote Perkins.

> And yet I suppose we must call it improved with its organized police, its halls of Justice, its lawyers' offices, library and printing office. . . . In fact, civilization [is] staring us in the face. We have now no rows, no fights, no murders, no rapes, no robberies to amuse us. Dr. Char-meaux yesterday pitched a Frenchman from a window of the first floor of the hotel to the street and we are so hard up for exciteable incidents, that even this little affair afforded some gratification.
>
> What with peaceable citizens, picayunish Yankees . . . , Jew clothing shops and down East strong minded

women, Sonora will soon be unbearable and all the old settlers will have to move off and seek more congenial shades.

Shortly after this, Perkins went to Argentina.

What was he to think, this forty-niner, he who had once walked miles to see a real live woman, when he read about the Y.M.C.A. Floral Festival: "The ladies stood so close that one walking through the crowd of them waded like him who walks through snow banks three feet deep." Girls sold ice cream and strawberries from flower-decked booths, and later the snowbanks of femininity, with gentlemen in formal broadcloth silhouetted among them like the black trees of winter, surged slowly toward the stage where a master of ceremonies whisked back a curtain to display the tableaux: "a vision of the Graces—living beauties standing in the classic attitudes of the marble group."

You can bet these living statues had proper clothes on, too. They had nothing in common with the troupe of "Model Artists" who came to San Francisco early in the rush. Those Model Artists were as undressed and suggestive as possible; even the forty-niners couldn't get used to them, or didn't care to, and they left the state under a cloud of disapproval and financial failure. But the prudent, decorous tableaux featured at bazaars and Floral Festivals were another matter: respectable and dull.

The crinoline set with its tea parties, luncheons, and festivals brought California the glimmer of Chinese lanterns in rustic gardens, the bustle of church activities, the rigid etiquette of the social call. The cotillion set inaugurated the Apollo Balls not many street numbers away from the blare of the fandango cellar, but light years away in essence. At Weaverville, Mrs. Edwards and a dancing master called the tune for the wild men of '49.

212

So he hadn't escaped, after all—this bearded barbarian in unwashed red flannel. Not unless he wanted to keep right on going down the rainbow—to the new Australian gold fields, to the Comstock silver rush, later to Montana, the Black Hills, or Tombstone, Arizona.

He couldn't slip off the rim of the civilized world as long as he could not escape that element in him which craved socks darned and bread properly baked, babies in the cradle and a sunbonnet girl who would get St. Peter to let him past those gates someday, in spite of his sins and his wanderlust.

CHAPTER *22*

Days of Jubilee

Naturally children—when there were children—lived for holidays and festivals; the argonauts—when there were no children, no sunbonnets, no church bazaars, just one big roaring camp —lived for Sunday.

Sunday was the main holiday in 1849. Back in civilization, Sunday was the day a man had to put on his best suit and take his family to church; he had to spend the remainder of the day in suitably quiet pursuits. It was a day of rest and drawn shades. But there were no shades to draw in the gold country, often no windows to draw shades over if there had been shades, and the forty-niner in his new-won freedom interpreted "day of rest" in his own peculiar fashion.

As one of them remembered:

> There were few of the miners who were religiously in-clined, yet they nearly all rested on the Sabbath, and the time was passed in wrestling, jumping, pitching horseshoes, playing cards, gambling, drinking whiskey, and so on.

There were giants in those hills: men who, after a long week of breaking backs over shovel, pick and pan, "rested" by wrestling and dancing and seeing who could jump the farthest.

The gold-rush style for Sundays was set before the forty-niners got there, and as one miner commented—recalling he had danced cotillions till after midnight, though it was Sunday night—"queer country—this California," but when in Rome you do as the Romans do. This classical excuse served all who came to the gold country and found the pattern as it was already established in 1848:

> The morals of the miners of '48 should here be noticed. No person worked on Sunday *at digging* for gold—but that day was spent in *prospecting* in the neighborhood, by the more sedate portion of the miners; while others spent it in playing at poker, with lumps of gold for checks; others, collected in groups, might be seen under the shades of neighboring trees, singing songs, playing at "old sledge" & drinking whiskey—in all of which proceedings, harmony, fun & good will to each other were the prominent features. We had ministers of the gospel amongst us, but they never preached. Religion had been forgotten even by its ministers.

They were busy prospecting, too.

This sounds very Arcadian, and apparently it was in '48 and most of '49. Rapidly the vendors of wild Sunday amusements rushed to this "anything goes" playground to dig their own fortunes with roulette wheel, liquor supply and professional feminine blandishments. The basic condition—Sunday as a fete day, not a religious day—remained the same, but the age-of-innocence air rapidly evaporated, good will was no longer the prominent feature, and with the addition of professional panderers, the amateur Sabbathbreaker lost his amateur standing and became an accomplished brawler and gambler.

Not suddenly, but gradually all over the state—first in the cities, later in the towns, still later up in the camps—the influence of churches and churchwomen began to spread over the Argonaut's Sunday. Women had always been the vestals preserving the church as an institution, and as they came first slowly and then abundantly into the gold country they brought this institution with them and set it down firmly as a visiting aunt sets her suitcase in the hall.

215

But California, with its long Spanish tradition of fiesta Sunday and its later stronger forty-niner tradition of hell-raising Sunday, never went completely back to the blue-law kind of Sunday current in some Eastern towns, even when councils passed blue laws. By 1860 Sunday was no longer the day when the majority of the population got blind drunk; neither was it any longer the day when the majority of the people had to wash socks, mend torn shirts, bake bread, and generally do up the household tasks for the week. There were women to do these jobs as they came up all week long; and there were women to see to it that men spent Sundays, if not in worship, at least in amusements that women could share.

So San Francisco families spent the day enjoying a Sunday drive in their carriages, out along the Mission Road, out past the Cliff House, taking Mama and the children to see the sea lions; or picnicking at Russ's Garden, or taking an excursion steamer to the Farallons. Sunday was still a fete day and so it remained; the compromise, for the more civilized sections, was church in the morning and fun in the afternoon. But Sunday wasn't bullfight day any more. If Mama conceded that it was all right to break the Sabbath and have a little fun, you had to have fun her way.

If the change in Sunday observance is an index to the taming of the forty-niner by his proper Victorian ladies, it is by the same token an index of the way California mores influenced those same ladies into a more tolerant and accepting attitude towards pleasure hunting. Changes in other holidays outline the same trend like numerous colored lines traced parallel upon a graph. The picture was further varied in two ways: Californians had a holiday all their own, and they learned to share in exotic holidays introduced by the large proportion of foreigners in their midst.

There was dancing in the streets of San Francisco on the night

216

of October 18, 1850. Lamps burned behind every window. From all the hilltops and from the islands of the Bay, bonfires blazed and rockets spattered triumphant trails of light, erasing the stars with the star dust of human jubilation.

San Francisco had just learned that California was admitted to the Union.

The steamship *Oregon* had scarcely docked before the news it bore was spreading all over the city, and messengers were steaming up the Sacramento to take word to the people of the interior. Eager hands hoisted a new flag up the Plaza's flagpole, with a new star added—the most important star—a star that stood out conspicuously white, brave and arrogant among the wind-weathered older stars.

Two cannon from the revenue cutter fired a salute: thirty-one guns—for the thirty-first state. Men heard it and left their monte game or rushed out of the theater to join the crowd in the streets and shake hands with cheering strangers. In every saloon the toast went round: To California and the Union; to California, the thirty-first state. Citizens gathered on the top of Howard and Green's building and danced on the roof until dawn sketched in gray the skyline of the city. Music from a hundred bands, laughter, impromptu parties: a radiance of gaslight, rockets, and champagne gaiety hung over San Francisco that night.

This, of course, was mere celebrating; it was not the official Celebration. That had to be carefully pre-arranged and carried off in style, weighty with pomp and circumstance. Admission Day was set for October 29, and during the evening of the eighteenth, while the town still roared its pleasure, promoters collected five thousand dollars to spend on a proper celebration complete with grand ball and formal ceremony. Like all set pieces of merrymaking, it wasn't nearly so hilarious as the spontaneous spree on that wild night of October 18.

217

Every year after that, Californians celebrated the shadow of the event on September 9, the anniversary of the date the nation's legal machinery had granted California the accolade of statehood. But the excitement of that day, when men leaped from the decks of the *Oregon* shouting the news, was never equaled by any other holiday.

The contributions of foreigners to the calendar of festivals were numerous and intriguing.

When the first gringos came, they watched with fascination the exotic fiestas of native Californians. One of the strangest was the hanging of Judas, during Holy Week.

> That evening I remember that a lot of Greasers made an effigy of Judas Iscariot to Jesus, stuffed with an old cocked hat, and a coat with a sagged pair of breeches stuffed with a lot of fire-crackers and powder so that the "traitor" Judas was blown to atoms . . . the "Greasers" half drunk with their excitement and "religion," brim full of bad whiskey, shouted for an hour.

Sometimes, the Mexicans would beg a passing party of Americans to shoot their Judas full of holes, and would scream and dance in a frenzy of revenge while the Americans obliged.

All the Catholic and Latin peoples celebrated all their saint's days, and non-Catholic Yankees used them as occasion to satisfy curiosity about heathen customs and express good will towards the foreigners by drinking with them. The same applied to patriotic celebrations imported from various nations.

The Chileños, commonest of South American immigrants, marked the anniversary of Chile's independence by organizing processions. Their parade was usually about two-thirds genuine patriots and one-third Yankees on the lookout for a good excuse to get drunk. One critic examined the results of chauvinism plus brandy and passed judgment that "though the Chileños reeled with a better grace, the Americans did it more naturally."

The California Germans, organized into pleasure-loving *Turnverein* Societies, had their special May festival. Yankees were admitted at twelve dollars apiece, which paid for all the heavy food and lager beer the guest could handle. At one such party the celebrants emptied sixty ten-gallon kegs of beer—"but it isn't intoxicating, you know." Nevertheless it must have helped, for it "was 240 feet to waltz around the room and we calculated that some of the Dutch Gals waltzed five miles in the course of the night."

On the seventeenth of March, all the Hibernian Societies turned out in full force, until the whole state seemed inundated by parading Sons of Erin decked out in green sashes. Once someone defiled the eve of the seventeenth by hanging an insulting effigy of St. Patrick at the top of the Plaza's liberty pole. This raffish dummy was draped in a bedraggled mass of many colored rags, had a sack of potatoes around his slack neck, and sported a whiskey bottle tied to one hand and a shillelagh wired to the other.

Furious Irishmen gathered the next morning at the foot of the pole, giving loud expression to the well-known Irish temper. Raging patriots made frantic efforts to climb the pole and tear down the insult. But the pole was rotten at the base and wouldn't bear even the weight of a thin calm Irishman. So in spite of police remonstrance, the crowd insisted upon chopping down the liberty pole and burning the effigy. They spent the rest of the holiday hunting the guilty party, uncertain whether to blame Mexican ragamuffins or the anti-Catholic Know-nothing party.

The French celebrated Bastille Day and other patriotic holidays. Sonora's William Perkins, always friendly with foreigners (he was one himself) went to one such party on February twenty-fourth but never did find out what they were celebrating. It was "a banquet in honor, I believe, of some republican triumph. . . . This present banquet was a socialist meeting and the walls of the room were hung around with a queer assemblage of names; amongst a host of others there were, Fourier, Robespierre, Jesus Christ, Moses, Spartacus, Franklin. . . ." And all present were busy damning Louis Napoleon.

While the Latin peoples kept their religious and national holidays, the Jews performed their ancient dignified rituals for Rosh Hashana and Yom Kippur, and the Chinese combined New Year's, Easter, and Fourth of July into one big explosion in January which they called New Year's Day. On this catchall festival, they put on new clothing and hung colored lanterns in front of their houses to honor their gods. Then as a kind of double-indemnity insurance against trouble, they turned ceremoniously toward Evil and banged gongs, exploded firecrackers, or set off rockets to frighten bad spirits clear out of the country.

The principal Yankee holiday was the Fourth of July. On this day all militia units, Volunteer Fire Companies, bands and fraternal organizations gathered to turn every Main Street into a grand parade. Streams of people wound through town and collected like creeks pouring into a reservoir at a central platform blazing with red, white and blue bunting, where the Orator of the Day would review the causes of the Revolutionary War and grow eloquent in apoplectic abuse of George the Third. The day had some aspects of an American hate festival like the Latin's Judas killing: the scapegoat was ceremoniously held up on the platform for everyone to vilify. Ordinary contemporary Englishmen were, of course, hospitably received— George III was the demon. After this oratorical orgy, another speaker read the Declaration of Independence.

At night, fireworks and bonfires lit every street corner, theaters held special patriotic programs and each town scheduled the maximum number of dinners and balls.

In the gold towns, the exigencies of frontier life sometimes altered the pattern. The dinner served to Iowa Hill celebrators one year had for its *pièce de résistance* a roasted grizzly. Dame Shirley was drafted to assist the Rich Bar celebration of 1853 by sewing together an American flag for the occasion. The program committee, enabled by the Dame's flying fingers to show forth the day's most precious symbol, were still painfully embarrassed by the fact that they couldn't perform the essential rite, the reading of the Declaration. There wasn't a copy in town.

During the fifties, a gradual shift in the principal emphasis of California holidays showed as on a relief map the altering of the social pattern from hell-raising frontier to American-Victorian community.

At the time of the gold rush, New Year's Day was nothing more than the signal for a record-breaking whiskey jag. New Year's Day never at any time became a temperance man's delight, but as the years passed a few frills were added to the dominant alcoholic motif. The day called for grand balls and formal dress, and society imported the custom of New Year's Day calls. In every home, women decked themselves out in company gowns of velvet and lace and laid out a long table with decanters, tumblers and assorted bottles. Frock-coated gentlemen strolled from door to door, taking care not to neglect a single lady in their little black books—to do so would have counted as a mortal insult. Many a congenial soul with a wide circle of feminine friends could barely stagger by the time he had drunk his way through his list.

Less favored gentlemen cheated by teaming up for their calls and visiting together the friends each had made separately. Unless the extra gentleman was well worth meeting, this practice was frowned upon by hostesses.

Because some gentlemen overdid the New Year's call business, there were hostesses who began to retrench. Some of them served only wine. Others went so far as to hang a basket outside the door for cards, indicating they were not at home and gentlemen could do the honors by dropping a card in the basket, getting no drink in return.

When San Francisco mud was particularly deep, men went calling in their high rubber boots. One exasperated matron kept a large bucket of water outside her door and insisted everybody wash his boots before he stepped into her parlor.

Towards the end of the fifties, California knew holidays that belonged rather to the quiet Connecticut towns and Pennsylvania valleys from which the pioneers had come than to the bonanza camps of '49. In February, stationery store windows sprouted valentines. And when May Day arrived, the public school children of San Francisco marched through the streets, the girls in white frocks carrying bouquets, or masqued as famous storybook characters. With a brass band leading the way, the youngsters romped across the city to Russ's Gardens, where they crowned their Queen, danced about the Maypole, gorged themselves on ice cream and held their annual party. This custom began quite early: in 1853 Soulé estimated there were a thousand children in the parade, representing seven schools.

In 1860, ferries bore four hundred children across the Bay to Alameda. There, with wild shrubs for a backdrop and a clump of elderberry bushes to mark entrance and exit, they presented plays and pageants, danced Highland flings and minuets, and sang ballads or patriotic tunes to an indulgent audience of parents and sisters, just as they do today for P.T.A. programs.

During that decade, Christmas observances changed as radically as a holiday could change.

222

The men of 1849 did the best they could with Christmas, but their resources were meager and peculiar. A miner recalled how he spent his first Christmas in the gold country. The dinner was the main thing, and everybody in camp agreed to co-operate in joint preparation of the feast. "We secured a loin of grizzly bear meat, some six scattered bottles of wine, and two pounds of raisins." Combining these with whatever supplies each could dig out of his regular larder, the gold diggers earnestly got to work mixing and baking. The masterpiece was turned out by a sea captain who had learned his business in a ship's galley: "a plum pudding made in ship fashion, and which he launched into a liquid so truly exquisite . . . as to leave one in doubt whether to prefer the pudding or the sauce." As there was no turkey, only grizzly, so there was also no sterling table service; when dinner was served, cooks turned into guests, wiped their bowie knives on their pants and pitched in.

Roast elk was another Christmas delicacy. Almost any kind of game would do. In the larger towns, Christmas of '49 was a day for eating, drinking too much, and carousing at masquerade balls and fandango cellars. Men who missed their families worst at this time and had to justify their desertion of home for El Dorado reacted by celebrating in extra-rowdy style that day.

Only a few years later, Sunday-school children were planting their Christmas trees in the middle of Musical Hall. By 1860, in the cities at least, the drunken bachelor's Christmas was largely replaced by the traditional family Christmas of roast fowl, gifts, and candlelit trees:

> By the piny odor about the market, by the fragrance of cedar in all the groceries, by the visions of innumerable boughs of evergreens, by the jolly cheers of schoolboys in the streets, by the apparitions of all manner of toys in the windows . . . we are made sure that Christmas is coming. The carts that creep slowly into town, or are whisked in at

express pace, are all loaded with Christmas trees. All the roads from the back country, and all the streets that lead from the ferries, smell of redwood and arbor vitae, which will bloom with gay flowers, and fruiten with all pleasant edibles, with dollars, and infinite baby gimcrackery, on Saturday evening next.

If the gold hunter shivering in his Happy Valley tent eleven years before, waiting his turn while the mug of rotgut was filled and passed or the bottle handed around from mouth to mouth, getting primed to go down to the Bella Union and buck the tiger or go roaring through Sydney Town hunting a woman—if he had been able to see this San Francisco Christmas of 1860, he could not have distinguished it from the Christmas of that other safe and comfortable world he had left three thousand miles behind him.

CHAPTER *23*

Vice Takes the Veil

This horrible picture, said to be truthfully drawn from real life . . . tells a sad tale; but, thank the Lord, "Babylon has fallen! has fallen!" and now above its scattered ruins the walls of the temple of virtue are towering, clearly defined in the sunshine of a better day . . . Men and women of sterling integrity and purity steadily withstood the desolating tide of licentiousness that swept over the land, often at the hazard of life; . . . until gambling was successfully put down by law throughout the state . . . and the whole fraternity of the "strange woman" has shared about the same fate.

—Evangelist William Taylor.

SO, ACCORDING TO THE STREET PREACHER, BABYLON BY THE GOLDEN GATE HAD FALLEN AT LAST, AND MORALITY WAS RAMPANT ALONG THE steep streets of the hoyden city. Virtue in a black dress with a neat white shawl had sailed in triumph through the Golden Gate; Virtue in a sunbonnet had crossed the plains and commandeered the cottages and started the big spring cleaning. While all proper Victorians hissed victoriously, the hussy El Dorado bowed her head and fled from the stage of California history.

How much truth was in the preacher's cry of triumph? Perhaps less than there was in the earlier stereotype that every man in California, from minister to Sydney cove, was a drunkard and a gambler. There was a portion of truth in both theories and in both, as in all oversimplifications, a great deal of pushing and pulling at the cloth of theory to make it cover the jagged uncompromising corners and unfinished jutting planks of fact.

225

So that we won't tear the cloth on the unexpected nails of historical fact—which to the great pain of historians, is seldom neat and tidy—it would be wise to look at the evidence on both sides of the question: Did womanly virtue tame the forty-niner, drive the strumpet spirit of El Dorado into exile?

It was certainly true that open gambling, the reigning pleasure of '49, was banned by the laws of 1855 and 1857 and after that disappeared from public view everywhere except in back streets and remote villages. Did this reform take place because of the coming of women, churches and conservative men whose public consciences were outraged by the spectacle of cities centering around gambling hells?

Women and other solid citizens certainly contributed their share to the business of pushing Vice back into the alleys. But the change arose from a whole complex of reasons, all fitting together, not from any single reason standing alone.

There was, for example, the matter of changing mood. In 1849 the spirit of the rush was the spirit of gambling in essence. As early as 1852, this spirit was no longer the dominant mood of the whole state. The atmosphere was still exciting and overstimulating. It continued to be. It was no longer autointoxicated.

Naturally, entertainers in other professions besides that of gambler and prostitute saw no point in leaving the golden fleece to be torn from the Argonaut by society's wolves. All kinds of pleasure vendors wanted their cut and hastened to win it. Within a couple of years, the forty-niner's plea that he had "nowhere to go" but hells and fandango cellars was a collapsed alibi, exploded by a profusion of balls, playgrounds, race tracks and theatricals.

During the mid-fifties the gambling houses and saloons were hit by blows from several directions at once. Not the least of these blows was the financial panic of 1854 and the depression that followed. California continued to be relatively extravagant, but the dream-world inflation of the early rush was over. The gambling fever naturally cooled as the sobering effects of deflation settled like smog upon the land. Many a prospector woke up with a headache and the knowledge that the golden days were gone.

Saloons continued to be numerous even for hard-drinking America of the fifties, but they could no longer count on a roaring trade by virtue of handing out anything alcoholic at a stiff price. They were heading into a buyer's market. They fought the decline of their overblown importance in every way possible to the promoter: they tried the free lunch and it proved a Frankenstein's monster; they introduced the novel idea of ventilation; they cut prices, led by Haney's Golden Gate with its "bit" plan. But nothing altered the trend.

The gold hunter of '49 was not necessarily a rich man. However, he thought of himself as Midas, because whatever he might have or have not at the moment, he confidently anticipated a rich strike in the near future. The Californian of 1853 might actually be a poor man, or he might own land, run a good business, jingle sufficient money in his pocket. But whatever his financial state might be, his mental state was different from the forty-niner's in one important respect: on the whole, he had returned to the land of reality. He still considered a drink necessary to the cementing of any business or social deal. But he did not consider it necessary to be irrationally lavish in the matter of drinks. And the temperance societies were moving in.

Between the hell-fire sermons of preachers and temperance societies and the embarrassing lack of ready cash or real expectations, many a Californian suddenly recalled his eternal soul and "people who never drank *water* before, have of late cultivated a hydropathic taste."

Reforms—or the outward appearance of reform—naturally appeared first in the larger cities. In the gold towns there was a certain lag. The people of Poverty Hill were beginning to get annoyed in 1858:

> For the last three Sundays, [a correspondent reported] the streets have been filled with drunken Indians, riding furiously and running races, to the great danger of all pedestrians, ladies and children in particular. To cap the climax, a saloon was opened with a brass band playing. The better portion of our citizens won't stand it much longer.

In the depression, the gambling hells faded more rapidly than the saloons, for in spite of lack of money hard liquor was the natural beverage of the average Westerner on his night out. But as there were more homes, there were fewer nights out. Although open gambling continued for a year or so after its peak fascination had passed, by 1855 the gambling industry was starved to a skeleton. As it was no longer the central vortex of California's night life, the legislators decided they could safely declare gambling a vice and pass laws against it.

Charles Ferguson, a forty-niner who defended the character of gamblers he knew, commented upon society's method of dealing with gambling:

> I abhor gambling in all places and in all forms, whether it be in mining regions or Wall street, or whether it be done at wholesale or retail. But society considers and treats gambling very much as it does the liquor traffic. It prosecutes and punishes the retailer and sends the distiller and brewer to the legislature and to congress. It legislates against betting on elections and horse racing as a bad and disgraceful business. But betting becomes respectable and legitimate when made on the price of wheat in Chicago, or railroad and mining stocks in New York. . . .

Ferguson was no doubt right. The antigambling law made it impossible for the Plaza to be lighted by the glow of its hells. It did this after the Plaza was no longer lighted in this manner because the hells no longer paid. It obviously did not touch the high-class gentlemen who gambled behind red plush drapes, nor the speculators out to make their millions in the gilded age. Neither, however—in spite of Ferguson's proletarian bitterness—did it touch the small-fry poker players in the back room of somebody's saloon in Red Dog or You Bet or Dead Man's Gulch. It merely put a rubber stamp upon society's decision, brought about by changing social and economic conditions, that wide-open gambling was no longer desirable in the urban centers of civilization.

The cleanup of prostitution posed a more delicate problem. Unlike gambling, which was a gold-frontier phenomenon and declined naturally with softening of gold-country tensions, the oldest profession was an ineradicable part of the Victorian system. Although its great influence was a manifestation of the early frontier's lack of women, and the influx of wives reduced this influence, nevertheless it was particularly dear to the anti-Puritan heart of the Argonaut. And the male-female balance in the population continued in the mining regions themselves to be six men to one woman, many of the women being, in Hittell's squeamish phrase, "neither maids, wives, nor widows." All contemporary observers made the comment over and over: the proportion of men to women was "unhealthy." This, combined with the Victorian social system, made prostitution a necessary part of the picture. The economy of scarcity also fostered various kinds of courting behavior toward all women, many of which were not the expression of unselfish gallantry.

Nevertheless, wives and mothers and solid citizens were swarming into the settlements the forty-niners and their camp followers had founded. In many cities and larger towns they were beginning to outnumber the adventurous element sufficiently to force through city councils ordinances suppressing fandango houses and brothels, as well as blue laws limiting Sunday pleasures.

These restrictive ordinances were always seconded by the cooperative police force with a spectacular roundup of all poverty-stricken, uninfluential, and unattractive streetwalkers.

The first San Francisco prosecution of a woman for being a prostitute was the trial and conviction of Johanna Maguire in 1858. It heralded a series of similar trials. In 1860, the police brought in Madame Mary Miller, whose worst sin was keeping a disreputable house in a reputable neighborhood and so causing several families to move away. For thus depressing real estate values Madame Miller spent three months in jail. Her trial was a test case and proved to the crusaders that it would be possible to purify large areas of the principal California cities.

The loud noises made by respectable citizens and the ready response of the police with a blustering show of token raids gradually had the intended effect. Prostitution was driven underground or segregated in districts where it would not offend the sensibilities of proper people. It continued to flourish in the wretched alleys of the slums and the cribs of Chinatown. The Chinese white slaves were particularly valuable for police raiding when raiding was required, but they were so numerous that raids had little real effect. The rich madames continued to prosper, though not quite so openly, and the Barbary Coast was right around the corner of history.

When respectable women became numerous enough to organize respectable parties, they had their own ways of dealing with the courted beauties from the wrong end of town.

Sarah Royce described a typical incident at the festival organized

230

by the church ladies to make money for a charitable society. Everything went well at the party until "there entered the room a man, prominent for wealth and business-power, bearing upon his arm a splendidly dressed woman, well known in the city as the disreputable companion of her wealthy escort. With cool assurance he proceeded to make her and himself quite at home; but in a few minutes he was waited upon by a committee of gentlemen," who told him the ladies managing the affair refused to receive his mistress and respectfully required him to take her home. He had boasted he could introduce Irene anywhere in the city, but the ladies showed him how wrong he was. San Francisco had changed.

Mary Jane Megquier commented in much less literary fashion:

> There is to be a soiree given by the ladies of the St. Francis which is said to be very select, there is quite a spirit of aristocracy prevailing here which in my opinion is composed of those that have been cramped in the states . . . but it is uncertain how they will succeed, at the last party they sent one home, she was taken there by an unsophisticated youth from Oregon. I think some one introduced him, to impose upon him, but he was so green he did not suspect any thing, although she kept a cigar and liquor store, but she was told the carriage was ready very soon after her arrival.

The lady was told that the carriage was ready; for ladies who passed out in the gutter, the policeman's wheelbarrow was ready and the station house received them for the night. One woman was arrested for joining the Easter parade in a costume which did not cover her above the waist. A civilized state, which California was rapidly becoming, could endure only so much from its raffish element. The exposed lady was not the only one. What could you do with a female like the one in the following news item, except arrest her for producing a riot?

231

She was at the time of the arrest in a state of extravagant elation and hilarity, cutting all sorts of capers and dancing in the streets.—She had as a sort of crowning ornament to her unearthly beauty a segar at least eight inches long stuck in her mouth at which she was pulling lustily, now and then puffing clouds of smoke from her mouth. She had entered half a dozen houses, and demanded a brandy smash or a cocktail, but each time a policeman carried her out without allowing her time to finish her potations; whereat she became frantic with rage and disappointment, and had to be taken to the Station House.

Certainly, Babylon had fallen. Alcoholics who could not contain their frustration when their drinks were snatched from them, prostitutes who had no influence and walked on the wrong street, ladies who wore no blouse or slept in the gutter—all these were swept off to jail.

And on the books of the state stood two laws which said No Public Gambling.

Everywhere rose churches, schools, temperance societies and benevolent societies. The society page was full of news about fetes and tea parties and church bazaars.

"The walls of the temple of virtue are towering," boasted the preacher.

But the evidence isn't all in. Not quite. If all of California no longer roared with raw and savage pleasures like a flaming wilderness, it nevertheless continued to simmer here and there in the corners; and sometimes that insidious gold-rush wildfire warmed hearths that in the East might have gone soberly cold.

CHAPTER 24

How Tame?

IN THE EARLY SIXTIES AN ENGLISHWOMAN VISITED CALIFORNIA AND, LIKE ALL TRAVELERS, WENT HOME AND WROTE A BOOK ABOUT IT. SHE acknowledged the marvels that reformers had wrought in the wilderness, but she added a small quibble:

> San Francisco, only a few years since the sanctuary of incorrigible rowdyism, is to-day one of the most orderly cities in the world. . . . Incredible as it may appear, San Francisco can fairly challenge the world for public decorum. It is asserted, *per contra,* that there exists within its precincts a frightful amount of private immorality.

Apparently the men of the gold rush, iconoclasts by nature, had absorbed certain basic attitudes that did not alter overnight with the appearance in their midst of virtuous women. "Notwithstanding the best efforts of a man," wrote William Perkins, "it is impossible not to be more or less infected by breathing continually a tainted moral atmosphere."

The Argonauts had seen few honest women in the early years. Some of them, even while they expressed a longing for the society of respectable females, must have formed the conclusion that there was no such thing as an incorruptible woman. Suffragette Eliza Farnham complained bitterly over disrespect to her sex: "The common expressions when women were spoken of, were that there was not an

233

honest one in the country—that those who professed to be so, were only greater hypocrites or more successful pretenders than the others —that none were entitled to respect, and that among men, only fools and dupes believed in them." Of course many of the forty-niners were embittered in the first place—that was one of the reasons men fled society for the stag culture of the Far West. Conditions they met there did not serve to restore their illusions about fair womanhood.

Against this lack of respect one must place the evidence of exaggerated chivalry. Often, however, this attitude led to the lavishing of compliments and gifts upon women who were not necessarily immune to the clink of nuggets.

Sarah Royce described and deplored the custom of "gentlemen manifesting their gallantry by expensive presents to their lady acquaintances. This seemed to be done at first in a sort of off-hand, jocular way." If a man made a rich strike, he wanted to boast about it; he therefore announced it to his lady with a "treat" which served to introduce the subject of his triumph. While some ladies refused these gifts, Mrs. Royce found that many joined in a kind of rivalry to see who could get the most. Singers and actresses counted it a bad night when no gifts were flung on the stage at the end of the show, and mothers of child stars bragged about the amounts their moppets received. Mrs. Royce shook her head over the corrupting tendency of this custom: "I have since seen some sad falls into positive vice of those whose downward course appeared to begin in these and similar practices."

Also, where stage and saloon entertainers were in great demand and extravagantly rewarded, almost any girl who was left stranded or who disliked drudging in the kitchen could get a singing and dancing job, and when she did, her surroundings were rarely encouraging to her virtue.

Almost every account of the gold rush contains at least one woman story indicating the "moral climate" of the time and the unscrupulousness of the predatory male. William Perkins told a sad tale about a gentleman expecting his wife from the East. Another gentleman found out the date of her arrival before the husband did and met her in his place, claiming the husband had asked him to guide her into the mountains. When she didn't arrive at her husband's cabin, the frantic husband began a search through the mountain towns. He ended up asking Perkins, who was a volunteer deputy, to lead a posse in search of the missing pair. Perkins shrugged his request off, expressing considerable sympathy for his bad luck, but maintaining this was a personal matter in which the law could not interfere. Privately, Perkins doubted very much if the interloper had been compelled to use force. In his opinion, while it was sad for the husband, the woman was probably perfectly happy. The story shows as much about the attitude of a Canadian "gone native" in Sonora as it does about typical scandals of the times.

"Nowhere is the sanctity of the domestic hearth so ruthlessly violated as in California," proclaimed sour Hinton Helper. His own view of basic female chastity differed hardly at all from the view which the violators used in self-justification:

> Female virtue . . . is known to be a very complex idea. There are women who are chaste only for want of the opportunity to be otherwise. There are others who are kept chaste by the force of public opinion . . . and the general fear of consequences; while a third class preserve their persons untainted by an innate purity of soul. . . . Many women, of conceded respectability in California, seem to have come out there for the exclusive purpose of selling their charms to the highest bidder. Others, of more honest hearts, have fallen victim to the peculiar seductions of the place. . . . [In spite of this, he concluded] Paradoxical

as the statement may sound, it is rigorously true that these very women have improved the morals of the community.

At least, they had made life more pleasant, less barbarous. Helper doubted if California contained many of his "pure" class, and he had absolutely no doubt that California had already corrupted all those of his other two classes.

To illustrate his point (he was writing in the early fifties), he stated that in a single week San Francisco courts had granted ten divorces, while at the same time only two marriages were recorded. And he passed on the sad story of an Englishman who told him that four years ago he and his wife had come to California with six other couples. Of these seven marriages, not one remained unbroken in 1853.

Some observers explained the highly breakable state of the marriage tie by claiming that in California any unhappy wife had no difficulty in discovering someone else who would be far kinder to her than her present mate, whereas in older communities this same wife might be just as unhappy but there would be nothing she could do about it.

Divorce laws were not scandalously lax. The California law, while milder than many Eastern ones, was stricter than the law of Indiana, which was at that time the Nevada of the United States.

John Hittell, who made one of the earliest attempts at compiling statistics on California, said, "No civilized country can equal us in the proportionate number of divorces." He lists 447 divorce suits begun in San Francisco in the years 1855–1860, most of which were granted; during 1860, eighty-five couples went into court. This hardly seems reason for crying havoc about the breakup of the American home. But set against the comparative scarcity of homes in the state and the much lower divorce rate in the East, it indicates

236

that the gold-rush urge for a freer life, while no longer running wild in general excesses, had not necessarily evaporated. On the contrary, it was soaking into the fabric of society.

Neither a Jeremiah like Helper nor a reveler like Soulé, Hittell attempted a sober estimate.

> In no part of the world, is the individual more free from restraint. Men, women, and children are permitted to do nearly as they please. High wages, migratory habits, and bachelor life, are not favorable to the maintenance of stiff social rules among men, and the tone of society among women must partake . . . of that among men, especially in a country where the women are in a small minority, and therefore are much courted.

As a restraining influence, public opinion was weak. The custom of the country permitted married women to go to parties with bachelor friends. Young girls went "into society" when they were about fifteen, and after that no one felt it necessary to chaperone them.

Compared to Victorian social conventions in general, California's looked like those of the Roaring Twenties even after the sunbonnet girls had established homes, promenades, ice-cream parlors, garden parties and church socials.

Mary Jane Megquier was a doctor's wife. She came to California with the doctor in 1849, leaving her children in the East with relatives. Her lively letters to her daughter showed clearly what California could do to a respectable woman eighteen years married, a lively and hard-working wife from a narrow provincial background.

At first, in September 1849, she wrote how insane the state was and how hard she was working keeping a boardinghouse:

I do not intend to stay only long enough to make a small pile of the dust which I am in hopes at the longest will not overrun two years. . . .

[November, 1849] Our motto is to make hay while the sun shines, we intend to sell the first good offer and return forthwith, although there are many things here that are better than in the states.

But she could not think of having her children come West because of the lack of schools. There were churches, but "it is all the same whether you go to church or play monte, that is why I like, you very well know that I am a worshipper at the shrine of liberty."

Five months after arrival, she had changed her mind about going home: she felt she could stay forever if only she had her children. She told why:

There is no scandal every one is his own man, not a word about such a thing is not respectable, you know I always detested that. . . .

[April, 1850] We had a nice little dance the other night. . . . I was engaged four dances ahead, isn't that smart? I suppose you will have a good laugh to see your Mother tripping the light fantastic toe.

After two years, the Megquiers went home to visit their children. In 1852 they came back to San Francisco, where Mary Jane continued to keep a boardinghouse. When the doctor became ill in 1854, they returned home to Maine. The next year Mary Jane was. back in San Francisco—alone.

[Nov. 29, 1855] The very air I breathe seems so free that I have not the least desire to return.

[Dec. 2] Mr. Jose wrote that your Father is very sick if he should be taken away it will only be what I have wished that might come upon myself, rather than live with one who was ever wishing me to sacrifice my health to his gratification. I endured it, I thought as long as I could, I know what the world will think of me. . . .

[Feb., 1856] Mr. Johnson of whom you often hear me speak is my gallant whenever I wish to go, he takes me to the mercantile lectures or any where I would like.

[March 19, 1856] I have been to a party at Mr. Johnsons . . . given in that new house he has been building. . . . We had strawberries put up in France, champagne in abundance.

Mary Jane had a drink from a glass holding hardly more than a tablespoonful and was delighted to discover it wasn't intoxicating. Mary Jane played euchre with the boys and went to quadrille parties. Mary Jane, married twenty-five years before, deserting her husband a year earlier and receiving news of her widowhood shortly after that desertion, was having the time of her life at last—except for missing her children.

Tough-minded and jaunty as she had become, she reacted to the rioting and threatened civil war that roused the city at the time of the 1856 Vigilance Committee with a note to her granddaughter:

I send you a picture as it is within one block of your grandmother it may please you. The carriage is the one the prisoner was taken in. Tell Scottie all about it, and instill into his little mind it is best to be good and not tease his sister.

The evolution of Mary Jane Megquier, though it concerns only one woman, typified what was going on in many different ways in the hearts of many other women. They too, like the Argonauts, were glimpsing a world not quite so tight and narrow and hedged as the world of quiet New England streets and back-country Ohio villages. Of course they could not countenance open licentiousness, brawling in the alleys, twenty-four-hour service at the monte table, and so they brought with them other amusements as bait to lure

239

the forty-niner from his roistering. No woman approves of a stag party unless she can attend it. Naturally, they wanted the men to have fun in their presence and therefore to have it their way. But they didn't frown upon a man's highly increased appetite for good times, and sometimes without realizing it they slipped into modified acceptance of his kind of pleasure hunting. No good woman drank —but Mary Jane sipped champagne in the house of her bachelor friend and found that nothing very dreadful happened. No good woman flirted—but Mary Jane and many like her discovered there was nothing to be gained by turning your back on an invitation to the theater just because the man who asked you wasn't your husband.

So while the good women used parties and theater engagements and home amusements to win their men back from the stag-party climate of El Dorado and tame him once more into a creature who would escort his wife to church and wear black broadcloth to the Floral Festival, they won a negotiated peace, not an unconditional surrender.

San Francisco society by 1860 was comparatively orderly and decorous. But the attitudes and the customs of Victorians-gone-native who kept order in that society were swayed slightly left of center by the winds of freedom blowing in the minds of men.

The domesticated forty-niner was glad to slip off his high boots and warm his feet at his own hearth and look with approval upon his wife sewing in the lamplight. But he had not forgotten the strumpet El Dorado. And sometimes he wished his sunbonnet girl was a little more like the hussy he had renounced for virtue's sake. He was not above seeing to it—a curl here, a flower there, a sip of champagne, a fling at waltzing in Russ's Garden—that his proper Victorian, while remaining a pillar of propriety at heart, acquired a few of the free-and-easy airs of El Dorado.

BIBLIOGRAPHY

BOOKS

ALVERSON, MARGARET BLAKE, *Sixty Years of California Song.* San Francisco: Sunset Publishing House, 1913.

ASBURY, HERBERT, *The Barbary Coast.* New York: A. A. Knopf, 1933.

AYERS, JAMES J., *Gold and Sunshine Reminiscences of Early Times in Southern California.* Los Angeles: Yarnell.

BANCROFT, HUBERT HOWE, *California Inter Pocula.* San Francisco: The History Company, 1888.

BARRY, T. A. and B. A. PATTEN, *Men and Memories of San Francisco in the spring of '50.* San Francisco: A. L. Bancroft, 1873.

BORTHWICK, J., *The Gold Hunters,* edited by Horace Kephart. New York, Outing Publishing Co., 1927.

BRISTOL, SHERLOCK, *The Pioneer Preacher.* Chicago: F. H. Revell Co., 1887.

BROMLEY, GEORGE TISDALE, *The Long Ago and the Later On.* San Francisco: A. M. Robertson, 1904.

BUCK, FRANKLIN A., *A Yankee Trader in the Gold Rush.* (Katherine A. Buck, compiler.) Cambridge, Mass.: Houghton Mifflin and Co., 1930.

BUSBEY, HAMILTON, *The Trotting and the Pacing Horse in America.* New York: The Macmillan Company, 1907.

CANFIELD, CHAUNCEY DE LEON, editor, *Diary of a Forty-Niner.* New York, San Francisco: M. S. Shepard Co., 1906.

CHRISTMAN, ENOS, *One Man's Gold—The Letters and Journal of a Forty-niner.* (Florence Morrow Christman, editor and compiler.) New York: Whittlesey House, 1930.

CLAPPE, MRS. LOUISE AMELIA KNAPP SMITH, *The Shirley Letters from California Mines in 1851–52.* (Reprinted from the *Pioneer Magazine,* 1854–55.) San Francisco, 1922.

CLELAND, ROBERT GLASS, *A History of California, The American Period.* New York: The Macmillan Company, 1930.

241

COAD, ORAL SUMNER and EDWIN MIMS, JR., *The American Stage* (Vol. XIV, *The Pageant of America Series*). New Haven: Yale University Press, 1929.

COLTON, WALTER, *Three Years in California*. New York: S. A. Rollo and Company, 1859.

COY, OWEN COCHRANE, *The Gold Days*. Los Angeles: Powell Publishing Company, 1929.

DANA, RICHARD HENRY, JR., *Two Years Before the Mast*. New York: The Macmillan Company, 1924.

DAVIS, WILLIAM HEATH, *Seventy-Five Years in California*. San Francisco: John Howell, 1929.

DRESSLER, ALBERT, *California's Pioneer Circus, Memoirs and Personal Correspondence Relative to the Circus Business*

DUDLEY, CHARLES M., *Sixty Centuries of Skiing*. Brattleboro, Vt.: Stephen Daye Press, 1935.

ELDRIDGE, ZOETH SKINNER, editor, *History of California*. New York: The Century Company, 1915. 5 vols.

FARNHAM, ELIZA W., *California, In-doors and Out*. New York: Dix, Edwards and Company, 1856.

FERGUSON, CHARLES D., *The Experiences of a Forty-Niner . . .* (Frederick T. Wallace, editor). Cleveland: Williams Publishing Company, 1888.

FISHER, EZRA, *Correspondence . . .* (Sarah F. Henderson, Nellie Latourette, and Kenneth S. Latourette, editors). [n. d., n. p.].

FROST, JOHN, *Incidents and Narratives of Travel in Europe, Asia, Africa and America in various periods of History*. Auburn and Buffalo: John E. Beardsley, 1852.

HALL, FREDERICK, *The History of San Jose and Surroundings*. San Francisco: A. L. Bancroft and Company, 1871.

HALLEY, WILLIAM, *The Centennial Year Book of Alameda County, California*. Oakland, California: William Halley, 1876.

HELPER, HINTON R., *Land of Gold*. Baltimore: H. Taylor, 1855.

HITTELL, JOHN S., *A History of the City of San Francisco and incidentally of the State of California*. San Francisco: A. L. Bancroft and Company, 1878.

HORNBLOW, ARTHUR, *A History of the Theatre in America from its Beginnings to the Present Times*. Philadelphia: J. B. Lippincott Co., 1919. 2 vols.

242

HUBBARD, W. L., editor, *History of American Music*. New York: Irving Squire, 1908.

HUNTER, GEORGE, *Reminiscences of an Old Timer*. San Francisco: H. S. Crocker and Company, 1887.

[HUNTLEY, HENRY V.], *California: Its Gold and Its Inhabitants*. London, 1856.

KIP, LEONARD, *California Sketches*. Albany: E. H. Pease and Company, 1850.

KNOWER, DANIEL, *The Adventures of a Forty-Niner*. Albany: Weed-Parsons Co., 1894.

KOBBÉ, GUSTAV, *Famous American Songs*. New York: Thomas Y. Crowell and Company, 1905.

KROUT, JOHN ALLEN, *Annals of American Sport* (Vol. XV, *The Pageant of America* Series). New Haven: Yale University Press, 1929.

LEACH, FRANK A., *Recollections of a Newspaperman*. San Francisco: Samuel Levinson, 1917.

LLOYD, B. E., *Lights and Shades in San Francisco*. San Francisco: A. L. Bancroft and Company, 1876.

MARRYAT, FRANK, *Mountains and Molehills, or Recollections of a Burnt Journal*. New York: Harper and Brothers, 1855.

MAY, EARL CHAPIN, *The Circus from Rome to Ringling*. New York: Duffield and Green, 1932.

MEGQUIRE, MARY JANE, *Apron Full of Gold*, edited by Robert Glass Cleland. San Marino: Huntington Library Press, 1949.

MEYER, CARL, *Bound for Sacramento*. (Translated from the German by Ruth Frey Axe.) Claremont, Calif.: Saunders Studio Press, 1938.

NEVILLE, AMELIA RANSOME, *The Fantastic City Memoirs of the Social and Romantic Life of Old San Francisco*. Boston: Houghton Mifflin Co., 1932.

PANCOAST, CHARLES EDWARD, *A Quaker Forty-Niner*. Philadelphia: University of Pennsylvania Press, 1930.

ROYCE, SARAH, *A Frontier Lady   Recollections of the Gold Rush and Early California*. (Ralph Henry Gabriel, editor.) New Haven: Yale University Press, 1932.

RYAN, WILLIAM REDMOND, *Personal Adventures in Upper and Lower California*. London: Parry and Company, 1852.

243

SAWYER, EUGENE T., *A History of Santa Clara County*. Los Angeles: Historic Record Company, 1922.

SOULÉ, FRANK, JOHN H. GIBSON, and JAMES NISBET, *The Annals of San Francisco*. New York: Appleton and Company, 1855.

TAYLOR, BAYARD, *Eldorado, or Adventures in the Path of Empire*. New York: George Putnam and Company, 1850. 2 vols.

TAYLOR, WILLIAM, *California Life Illustrated*. New York: Carlton and Porter, 1858.

TAYLOR, WILLIAM, *Seven Years of Street Preaching*. New York: Phillips and Hunt, 1856.

UPHAM, SAMUEL C., *Notes of a Voyage to California . . . Together with Scenes in El Dorado in the Years 1849–50*. Philadelphia: *n. n.*, 1878.

WILLIAMS, MARY FLOYD, *History of San Francisco Committee of Vigilance of 1851*. Berkeley, California: University of California Press, 1921.

WILSON, LUZENA S., *Luzena S. Wilson, Forty-Niner*. Mills College: The Eucalyptus Press, 1937.

WOODS, DANIEL B., *Sixteen Months at The Gold Diggings*. New York: Harpers Brothers, 1851.

WOODS, JAMES, *Recollections of Pioneer Work in California*. San Francisco: Joseph Winterburn and Company, 1878.

CALIFORNIA NEWSPAPERS 1848–60

DOWNIEVILLE, Calif. *Mountain Echo*
MARYSVILLE *Herald*
MARYSVILLE *Weekly California Express*
SACRAMENTO *Daily Union*
SAN FRANCISCO *California Home Journal*
"   "   *California Police Gazette*
"   "   *California Star*
"   "   *Californian*
"   "   *Call*
"   "   *Daily Alta California*
"   "   *Daily Evening Picayune*
"   "   *Daily Herald*
"   "   *Golden Era*
"   "   *Pacific News*

244

SAN FRANCISCO *Pictorial Town Talk*
"   "   *Sun*
"   "   *Weekly Alta California*
SONORA *Herald*

MANUSCRIPT STATEMENTS IN BANCROFT LIBRARY
UNIVERSITY OF CALIFORNIA

ARMSTRONG, WILLIAM, " '49 Experiences."
AYERS, F. H., "Personal Adventure."
BACON, L. W., "Memoirs."
BARSTOW, ALFRED, "Statement."
BARTLETT, WASHINGTON, "Statement."
BOGGS, WILLIAM, "Reminiscences."
BORTHWICK, "California."
CASSIN, "Statement."
CHAMBERLIN, J., "Statement."
CONWAY, JOHN, "Early Days."
FAY, CALEB T., "Statement of Historical Facts on California."
FINDLA, "Statement."
GREEN, ALFRED A., "Life and Adventures of a 47'er."
GRIMSHAW, WILLIAM R., "Narrative."
HAWLEY, DAVID N., "Observations."
LITTLE, JOHN T., "Statement."
MERRILL, ANNIS, "Statement."
MOORE, AUGUSTUS, "Pioneer Experiences."
PERIERA, FERNANDEZ, "Statement."
PERKINS, WILLIAM, "Journal."
PIERCE, HENRY H., "Rough Sketch."
RICHARDSON, "Experiences."
ROACH, "Statement."
SAWTELLE, C. M., "Pioneer Sketches."
SCHMIEDELL, "Statement."
STAPLE, "Statement."
SUTTON, O. P. "Statement."
SWAN, JOHN H., "A Trip to the Gold Mines of California."
VAN DYKE, WALTER, "Statement."
WILLIAMS, "Statement."
WINAN, JOSEPH W., "Statement of Recollections."